OAKLAND COMMUNITY COLLEGE
3 2355 00106126 6
KF 3941 .F74 1989
OCHL
The privilege

THE PRIVILEGE TO KEEP AND BEAR ARMS

Recent Titles from Quorum Books

Private Pensions and Employee Mobility: A Comprehensive Approach to Pension Policy
Izzet Sahin

Group Decision Support Systems for Effective Decision Making: A Guide for MIS Practitioners and End Users
Robert J. Thierauf

Deregulation and Competition in the Insurance Industry
Banks McDowell

Chemical Contamination and Its Victims: Medical Remedies, Legal Redress, and Public Policy
David W. Schnare and Martin T. Katzman, editors

Statistics for Real Estate Professionals
Rebecca F. Guy and Louis G. Pol

Decision-Aiding Software and Legal Decision-making: A Guide to Skills and Applications Throughout the Law
Stuart S. Nagel

Regulatory Interventionism in the Utility Industry: Fairness, Efficiency, and the Pursuit of Energy Conservation
Barbara R. Barkovich

The Acceptance of Human Resource Innovation: Lessons for Management
Ellen Ernst Kossek

Doing Away with Personal Injury Law: New Compensation Mechanisms for Victims, Consumers, and Business
Stephen D. Sugarman

International Transfer Pricing Policies: Decision-Making Guidelines for Multinational Companies
Wagdy M. Abdallah

THE PRIVILEGE TO KEEP AND BEAR ARMS

The Second Amendment and Its Interpretation

WARREN FREEDMAN

Q QUORUM BOOKS
New York • Westport, Connecticut • London

Library of Congress Cataloging-in-Publication Data

Freedman, Warren.
The privilege to keep and bear arms : the second amendment and its interpretation / Warren Freedman.
p. cm.
Bibliography: p.
Includes index.
ISBN 0-89930-411-7 (lib. bdg. : alk. paper)
1. Firearms—Law and legislation—United States. I. Title.
KF3941.F74 1989
344.73'0533—dc 19
[347.304533] 88-38312

British Library Cataloguing in Publication Data is available.

Library of Congress Catalog Card Number: 88-38312
ISBN: 0-89930-411-7

First published in 1989 by Quorum Books

Greenwood Press, Inc.
88 Post Road West, Westport, Connecticut 06881

Printed in the United States of America

The paper used in this book complies with the Permanent Paper Standard issued by the National Information Standards Organization (Z39.48-1984).

10 9 8 7 6 5 4 3 2 1

Contents

Preface

Whether you favor or reject the right or the privilege to keep and to bear arms within the meaning of the Second Amendment to the U.S. Constitution, this single volume will excite you, because it frankly presents the case for the anti-gun, anti-weapon, or anti-arms enthusiast. Here are answers to the arguments set forth by the National Rifle Association and its satellites of members and of arms dealers who have products to sell. The Second Amendment is carefully annotated, word by word, and the historical background thereto is nevertheless delineated as objectively as possible.

The fourth chapter deals with the courts and their interpretation of the Second Amendment. Limitations on the privilege or right to keep and bear arms are examined under the police power of the states and of the federal government. Next is an analysis of legislation dealing with gun control, both federal and state. The seventh chapter is intriguing, for here are the essentials of *civil* liability on the part of gun manufacturers, gun distributors, and dealers in firearms and guns. What happens when the victim who is shot decides to sue person or persons like gun manufacturers, other than the assailant with the gun? The theory of "negligent entrustment" provides a basis for legal action by the victim of the gun assault; products liability law also takes over, as does the strict liability concept of the dram shop acts, which hold the bartender strictly liable for injuries, death, or damages for selling liquor to an intoxicated person. Chapter 8 looks to the future of the gun debate. Again, whether you agree or dispute the contents of this dynamic single volume, you'll appreciate the disclosing of the arguments and the timeliness of the material.

THE PRIVILEGE TO KEEP AND BEAR ARMS

1

The Political and the Economic Elements of Firearm and Gun Control

1.1 INTRODUCTION

Only a decade or so ago it might have been said in all truth that there was virtually no informed debate on a scholarly level about firearms and gun control.[1] Most observers recognized the political and economic obstacles to the enactment of effective gun control (designed to restrict civilian ownership of firearms and guns); nevertheless, a vast majority of people favored gun control measures that would remove firearms and guns from civilian hands. Today the very underpinnings of restrictions on civilian ownership of firearms and guns are under attack, principally by the political Right and by the powerful lobby of the National Rifle Association. By the same token the number of advocates of control over firearms and guns has increased, particularly in view of the acknowledged fact that there are more firearms and more guns on the street, concomitant with the ever-increasing violent crime that has become an accepted relevant fact in the later 1980s.[2] "Crime in the streets" has become a national obsession; unfortunately, too many politicians have cried out for "law and order" without any true appreciation of the need to restrict, not increase, the number of such weapons available. The political reaction of encouraging the average civilian to protect himself or herself with firearms and guns was not the answer. Statistics reveal that the number of armed robberies jumped from 138,000 in 1965 to 376,000 in 1972, while murders committed with firearms and guns shot up from 5,000 to 11,000 in the same period of time.[3] The figures for the late 1980s are too shocking to reveal with any accuracy; it is sufficient to point out that the number of firearms and guns in the United States today exceeds 120 million.[4] The economic impact is seen in the fact that the average firearm or gun sells for $75.00, so that the present firearms and gun stock is worth approximately $9 billion. The Insurance Information Institute points out that injuries associated with ladders send about 90,000 persons to the hospital each year; that 70,000 persons are each year injured from use of lawnmowers, and about 45,000 are injured annually from using power saws.[6] The enormous volume of injuries and deaths from the use of firearms and guns simply cannot be compared with such common household products that also can cause injuries and deaths. The assassinations of President John F. Kennedy, Martin Luther King, and Robert F. Kennedy, and the attempts on the lives of Presidents Gerald Ford and Ronald Reagan only serve to emphasize the hazard of firearms and guns in the hands of too many persons. The philosophy that guns don't kill, only people kill, belies the fact that people don't readily kill without firearms and guns!

The volatility of the gun control issue is seen in excerpts from editorials in the *Washington Post,* the *New York Times, Newsday Mazagine,* and the singular statement of U.S. Senator Alan K. Simpson of Wyoming:

Gunrunners' Sneak Attack

It's been a busy summer for the master gun-worshippers of the National Rifle Association—whose troops have been all over Capitol Hill, methodically whipping up an ugly legislative surprise for all who believe in reasonable controls on handgun traffic. The NRA threat this year is double-barreled: If unchecked, it would mean (1) the end of almost all *existing* federal regulations of guns, and (2) a go-ahead for handgun purchases by certain convicted felons and for free-wheeling interstate traffic in all sorts of pistols, machine guns and other firearms that can hardly be considered as sporting equipment. . . .

Whatever the comouflage, people shouldn't be fooled by this destructive legislative attempt to repeal the reasonable minimum gun controls that do exist. The 1968 Gun Control Act, which the NRA would repeal, was enacted after the assassinations of Robert F. Kennedy and the Rev. Dr. Martin Luther King, Jr., to put basic safety rules on the books: Licensing of gun dealers, bans against certain types of weapons such as machine guns, prohibitions against sales to out-of-state residents and against gun trafficking by convicted felons.

None of this has, or would, disarm the sportsman. National polls have shown time and again that a solid majority of Americans support federal handgun controls to place some responsibility on handgun ownership and handgun commerce. If thoughtful legislators respect this desire, and if they stop listening to a narrow special-interest lobby, the scant controls now on the books can be preserved. (*Washington Post,* September 3, 1980)

Dealer in Illegal Guns: Businessman Thriving In Flourishing Market

Once a month, an inconspicuous late-model rented station wagon drives into Manhattan loaded with neatly stacked cardboard boxes. In the boxes, according to a gun dealer named Sam Yang, are brand-new revolvers and semi-automatic pistols.

For nearly 10 years, one of Mr. Yang's employees has made the short trip to Pennsylvania, Vermont or other nearby states—to pick up the dealer's monthly shipment. Last year, by his own rough calculations, Mr. Yang realized nearly $100,000 from his thriving business.

He did not, however, report this income to tax authorities, for he is an illegal gun dealer, hijacking arms shipments and transporting guns across state lines and selling them without a license.

Mr. Yang (a pseudonym) and other illegal dealers are the core of a tight network that the police estimate has flooded New York City with two million illegal handguns to date. He regards himself as typical: "I'm a distributor," he said. "I'm the average Joe who's doing it."

And, he said, New York State's new gun-control law, which imposes stiffer penalties for illegal sale or possession of unlicensed handguns, will have little effect on his business. "There is always a market for guns," Mr. Yang said. (*New York Times,* June 16, 1980)

Gun Decontrol in Congress

The National Rifle Association shells out plenty of campaign contributions, but the pro-gun forces are so strong in some parts of the country that money isn't needed to make congressmen timid about trying to control handguns. One congressional staff member estimates that fully one-third of the votes in his western district turn on the gun issue alone.

For the first time in years, the chances of meaningful handgun legislation are so poor that the NRA isn't even concentrating on fighting it. Instead, it's pushing a bill that would further erode the already pitifully ineffective federal gun control laws. Last month, the NRA got powerful support from the Republican platform, which states:

"We believe the right of citizens to keep and bear arms must be preserved. Accordingly, we oppose federal registration of firearms. . . . We . . . support congressional initiatives to remove those provisions of the Gun Control Act of

1968 that do not significantly impact on crime but serve rather to restrain the law-abiding citizen in his legitimate use of firearms.''

That's shorthand for making it easier to ship and sell handguns across state lines, making it harder to convict people accused of violating the federal handgun laws and making it possible for people convicted of federal felonies to own guns. (*Newsday,* August 11, 1980)

Statement of Senator Alan K. Simpson of Wyoming

I appreciate the opportunity to make a very brief comment on gun control. I have always been opposed to any form of gun control or registration. The United States Constitution guarantees the right of the people to keep and bear arms in Article II of the Bill of Rights. To me that says it all.

Having practiced law for many years, I know that there is always ''another side.'' We have all heard a string of horror stories involving firearms—all kinds of firearms, not just so-called ''Saturday night specials.''

Just like all other forms of freedom, the right to keep and bear arms leads to specific evils in specific circumstances. In America we have chosen to provide maximum freedom in the belief that the net overall effect is positive. Once the principle of gun control is accepted, we can only argue expediency—that the line should be drawn one place rather than another, on the basis of inevitably limited perspectives. We cannot ever be fully aware of all the direct and indirect results of what we do. The obvious short-term effects of an action can too frequently make it appear beneficial even when the actual long-term result, considering indirect as well as direct effects, is quite harmful.

Gun control is a tough, gut-hard issue in my part of the country. It is crystal clear what the feelings of my constituents are on this issue. I share those feelings. (Hearings before the Subcommittee on the Constitution of the Committee on the Judiciary, U.S. Senate, September 15, 1980 (Serial No. 96–83) at 371)

A word on ''lobbying'' by pro-gun and anti-gun groups: according to the *New York Times* (August 23, 1988) at page A18, the National Rifle Association expended in 1987 $668,058, the Gun Owners of America, $608,672, and the Citizens Committee for the Right to Keep and Bear Arms, $271,435, for a total of $1,548,165. The sole lobbying group supporting restrictions on firearms, Handgun Control, Inc., spent $900,343. Hence, more than $2 million was reported to have been spent by four lobbying organizations concerned with firearms. But these figures do not encompass unreported expenditures, ranging from high salaries paid to executives to the numerous expenses attendent to tangential activities of these propaganda groups. Then, too, other organizations have contributed portions of their overall expenditures for or against firearms legislation and these amounts are not identifiable as firearms expenditures. The bottom line is simply that too much money goes into the hopper for firearms, pro and anti!

1.2 THE CONFLICTING VALUES

It has been stated that firearms legislation and firearms litigation represent conflicting values between urban and rural communities.[7] Before World War II, America was largely a rural society with deep-rooted values based on property ownership and self-defense. Any tampering with these "rights" brought forth a profound response; rural America answered, "God created men—Samuel Colt made them equal." Firearms and guns, however, are not "tools" for carrying out such mandates; firearms and guns, it is submitted, are instruments of injury and death. Firearms and guns are dangerous instruments in the hands of too many people and with a potential for destruction that far exceeds the technical competence necessary to employ them.

Politically speaking, the values of rural America literally argued that outlawing firearms and guns means that only the government will have firearms and guns. Anarchy would be prevented, but then an urban mob would control the country, and that logical argument was appealing to owners of firearms and guns. The impact of that view of the rural-urban conflict is further evident in the fact that thirty-nine States have constitutional provisions relating to the "right to keep and bear arms."[8]

Arms control on the international front among nations is similarly difficult. Little effort has ever been made to control the manufacture, distribution, and use of death-dealing small arms in most countries around the world. It is apparent that it is fear and fear alone that is the mother of firearms and guns. Yet the Hague Conference of 1899 had prohibited so many years ago high-velocity ammunition, or dum-dum bullets, in international warfare; and this prohibition is found in 36 Stat 2277, enacted by the U.S. Congress in 1909 (61st Congress). Obviously, the thrust of this international prohibition fell on deaf ears throughout the world. It should be observed that in no other country in the world have firearms and guns so materially altered the course of history as in the United States.[9] In the political arena president after president has had his life shortened by a concealable gun; spectacular assaults and murders with firearms and guns have affected the economy through the deaths of labor leaders, corporate heads, police, and other dominant people in industry. There is rarely a person who has not had an experience or who does not know someone who has had a personal experience at the wrong end of a firearm or gun. The problem is not localized or confined to metropolitan areas; the least violent regions have been combat zones as people with guns have gone on the rampage.

1.3 THE RELATIONSHIP BETWEEN VIOLENCE AND THE AVAILABILITY OF FIREARMS AND GUNS

The prime question is sometimes phrased in terms of why society at large wants to regulate firearms and guns, and the answer appears to concern the relationship between violence and the availability of firearms and guns.[10] It is suggested that there are three ways in which the availability of firearms and guns might increase crime and violence: (1) assault-instigating effects, that is, the possibility that the mere sight of a firearm or gun, or the possession of a firearm or gun, could trigger an assault that otherwise would not have occurred;[11] (2) crime-facilitating effects, in other words, the possibility that the possession of a firearm or gun may make possible or make easier the commission of a crime that a criminal had wanted to commit but might not have committed but for the availability of the firearm or gun;[12] and (3) assault-intensifying effects, or the possibility that when an assault occurs, for whatever reason and in whatever circumstances, the use of a firearm or gun increases the severity of any resulting injuries or death, compared to what would have occurred had the likely substitute weapon such as fists, brass knuckles, or even a knife been employed.[13]

Most recently, ''toy guns'' have occupied the attention of parents and psychologists who wonder if playing with toy guns and other war toys encourages violent behavior among youngsters or inures them to the horrors of death and war. Government officials are also concerned, and the state of Connecticut recently outlawed the manufacture or sale of realistic toy guns.[14] Do we as a nation take the subject of guns, toy or real, much too cavalierly? Scientific testing confirms that we do, as attested by the following research results:

The most frequently cited research was conducted in 1976 by Charles W. Turner and Diana Goldsmith, psychologists at the University of Utah. Children were observed playing with neutral toys like blocks and airplanes and then with toy guns. The researchers found that the children exhibited more physical and verbal aggression after playing with guns.

In 1985, Dr. Thomas Radecki, a psychiatrist and the executive director of the National Coalition on Television Violence, an advocacy group based in Illinois, studied 20 preschoolers. He compared the effects of playing with He-Man and Masters of the Universe figures, and playing with Cabbage Patch dolls. Dr. Radecki said the incidence of antisocial and violent behavior doubled after the youngsters played with the violent-theme toys. "The evidence is quite strong that we are transmitting an unhealthy message encouraging children to have fun pretending to murder each other," he said. . . . Dr. Lee Salk, a professor of psychology, psychiatry and pediatrics at the New York Hospital-Cornell Medical Center, agreed, noting that the very nature of aggressive play has changed over the years. Children, he said, once played with "little tin soldiers built around heroic elements in our history." By contrast, "today we have Rambo vigilantes who are not responsible to authority." "The message of toy guns," Dr. Salk concluded, "is that you solve problems by pulling a trigger."

Stevanne Auerbach, a psychologist and the director of the San Francisco International Toy Museum at the Cannery, said she would ban all toy guns because children accustomed to playing with them have played with real weapons left out by adults, sometimes with tragic results.[15]

There appears to be, however, no *conclusive* evidence of such a relationship between the availability of the firearm or gun and the criminal violence. The presumption and the probability is that the relationship is genuine and reliable, but not in all instances nor under all circumstances. Nevertheless, society's perception favors the causal relationship, and, for pragmatic purposes, that perception controls. The *New York Times* (November 18, 1988) editorial, headed "Guns Do Kill People," describes a 1988 study published in *The New England Journal of Medicine* that examined gun and crime records in Seattle and Vancouver, two cities that are similar in population as well as in geography, climate, and history, that share similar rates of education, income, and unemployment: "The two cities differ dramatically, however, in their approach to guns. Vancouver restricts purchasers of handguns to legitimate target shooters and collecters, and severely limits their use. Seattle allows virtually unrestricted over-the-counter sales and requires only a permit to carry a concealed gun on the street. Not surprisingly, gun ownership is more than three times greater in Seattle than in Vancouver." The editorial then states that "researchers analyzed aggravated assaults and homicides according to the weapons used. The results were striking: the rates of crimes committed with knives and other weapons were roughly the same in both cities, but the rates of crimes committed with guns were far greater in Seattle. In fact, the gun crimes appeared to account almost entirely for Seattle's higher rates of aggravated assaults and homicides.'' And the editorial concludes: ''Most homicides begin not with crimes but with arguments that turn ugly. With guns readily at hand, they are more likely to turn deadly as well.''

1.4 THE LEGISLATIVE ROLE

With the possible exception of abortion there is no area of the law that has aroused more controversy in this century than firearms and guns legislation.[16] Legislatures reflecting the will of the people seek to counteract the alarming increase in violence caused by firearms and guns. Unfortunately, too many legislative measures reflect a combination of diverse opinions regarding effective methods of gun control and varying degrees of sensitivity toward the concerns of gun owners. Another complicating factor is that federal, state, and local levels of government enact such legislation, and different communities have strikingly different problems and different demands.[17] One appropriate municipal example is found in the total ban on handguns enacted in Morton Grove, Illinois, in 1982;[18] the ordinance was approved by both the federal district court for the Northern District of Illinois and by the Seventh U.S. Court of Appeals.[19] But the San Francisco City ordinance was at the same time held void on the grounds that it conflicted with legislation enacted by the state of California and that it concerned an area expressly preempted by state legislation.[20]

Among the many legislative considerations in enacting firearm and gun control statutes or ordinances are (1) effectiveness of the legislation, and (2) the cost of such legislation.[21] Effectiveness or efficacy is difficult to measure, not only because of the lack of national or even state uniformity, but because of the prevalence of local regulations, which frequently impose more stringent requirements than federal or state laws.[22] For example, Washington, D.C., has what appears to be a strict handgun registration law, but it is easily bypassed by traveling a few miles to neighboring Virginia or Maryland to procure a handgun.[23] The cost of gun control focuses upon the major expense of registration and licensing; the cost varies with the thoroughness of the background investigation of the potential licensee and the extent to which records are computerized, as well as the sheer number of licensees and registrants.

Legislatures reflecting the will of the people discern public opinion from letter volume and public opinion polls. Letter volume is hardly reliable, since any dedicated group of persons can instigate "bullet votes," provided the group has the financial resources to conduct such a one-sided campaign. Public opinion polls offer more reliable data on the desires of the public at large, but again there are incredibly large errors in the interpretation of such polls.[24] A significant expression of public opinion is often related to the election or rejection of legislators themselves.

1.5 TOTAL BAN ON FIREARMS AND GUNS

On May 23, 1988, the state of Maryland enacted legislation, effective January 1, 1990, making it illegal in Maryland to sell or manufacture pistols that a special nine-person board determines are easily concealed, inaccurate, unsafe, or poorly made.[25] But it will not be illegal to own such weapons commonly described as "Saturday Night Specials." Interestingly, statistics show that during the past twenty years such pistols have been used to kill 250,000 people and to injure 1,500,000 others.[26] But the Maryland ban on pistols and the Morton Grove ban on handguns are but an infinitesimal part of the problem of the widespread availability of firearms and guns, and a total ban on all firearms and guns is a wholly different matter.

A persistent and emotional issue is the fear that a total ban will lead to confiscation[27] and will sound the death knell for the lucrative gun business, which is worth more than $10 billion.[28] On the other hand, the continued existence of an unwarranted supply of firearms and guns (estimated at 120 million) is an underlying factor in the decline of major urban centers, the so-called inner cities where use of guns is a way of life. Confiscation of all firearms and guns might very well come within the Fifth Amendment's mandate that private property cannot be "taken for public use" without just compensation.[29] The thrust here is that the benefited public as a whole must pay for whatever individual property rights are destroyed or diminished, unless the possession of the property in the first place was illegal.[30] As Justice Oliver Wendell Holmes said more than sixty-five years ago, "Government hardly could go on, if to some extent, values incident to property could be diminished without paying for every such change in the general law.''[31] The tests of confiscation embrace such factors as physical appropriation and diminution in value, together with validity of governmental authority, as revealed in the exercise of police power and eminent domain.[32] But the true test regarding payment of compensation is the nature of the governmental use of the confiscated property and not necessarily the resulting benefit to the public. Yet in United States v. Caltex (Philippines) Inc.[33] the U.S. Supreme Court observed that the federal government had destroyed oil reserves and facilities to avoid their falling into the hands of the Japanese during World War II. While the federal government paid for the oil destroyed, the Court upheld the government's refusal to pay compensation for the destruction of the facilities: in wartime the destruction of private property must be ``borne by the sufferers alone.''[34] In liquor prohibition cases the government has been upheld in not paying compensation when state or federal law represented an exercise of the valid police power.[35] Thus, a state or federal government could declare all firearms and guns to be an evil to be avoided for the benefit of the public, and no compensation would be required for confiscation of the firearms and guns under several theories, including the noxious use test.[36]

1.6 EXCEPTIONS TO TOTAL BAN ON FIREARMS AND GUNS

Obviously, any total ban on firearms and guns must take into consideration important exceptions, both in terms of kinds of firearms and guns and in terms of those persons who use those firearms and guns. For example, the following persons must be excepted from the total ban: police officers,[37] wardens and other jail or penitentiary personnel, members of the active and reserve armed forces and National Guard, special agents employed by railroads or public utilities to perform police functions, guards of armored car companies, watchmen and security guards actually or regularly employed in the commercial or industrial operation for the protection of persons employed and private property related to such commercial or industrial operation, licensed gun collectors, possessors of antique firearms and guns, among others.

Even strict firearms and guns control laws appear to make exceptions for ``long guns,'' which are difficult to conceal and therefore unlikely to be used in the commission of crime. However, long guns are much more deadly than handguns and can still be used to commit crimes and perhaps "settle arguments," so that the exception is not fully warranted.

1.7 NECESSITY FOR LICENSING AND REGISTRATION OF FIREARMS

The Bureau of Alcohol, Tobacco, and Firearms (BATF) of the U.S. Treasury Department is responsible for federal licensing and registration of guns and other firearms. According to BATF records, licensing efforts have proved ineffective; BATF issued over 1.5 million licenses between 1969 and 1978, for example, and found grounds to deny less than 0.75 percent of applicants and to revoke an infinitesmal 0.007 percent of licenses during that period.[38] The National Firearms Registration and Transfer Record consists of two separate filing systems. In the first, each registered possessor of a firearm has an individual file containing a copy of the original registration form for each and every firearm in that person's possession. Second, an index card file provides both a backup and a crosscheck for the file. Both components are examined in searches for evidence.

The prime focus of licensing and registration has been on concealed weapons, including such items as knives, blackjacks, slingshots, brass knuckles, and handguns.[39] State and local licensing and registration is illustrated by the recent New York decision in Matter of Teich, where the county brought a proceeding to revoke the respondent's pistol license after the respondent had pleaded guilty to trespass in satisfaction of petit larceny charges.[40] But the court observed that the offense to which the respondent pleaded quilty was not a felony or serious offense as described in the New York Penal Law; the court also noted that the county produced no evidence that respondent had ever misused the pistol. Accordingly, the court denied the revocation application by the county.[41]

Licensing systems may be classified as permissive, restrictive, or permissive-restrictive.[42] In a permissive licensing system anyone not in a prohibited class of persons will be issued a license to possess a firearm and gun. For example, in the state of Washington the statute provides that a license must be issued unless the applicant has been convicted of a crime of violence or is a drug addict or a habitual drunkard, or has been confined to a mental institution.[43] A restrictive licensing system is illustrated by the New York statute, which requires an affirmative showing of need and good moral character, even for nonprohibited individuals, before a license or permit will be issued.[44] New Jersey and Massachusetts employ the permissive-restrictive licensing system.[45]

The primary objective of a registration system, in contrast to licensing that focuses on the individual owner of firearms and guns, is the maintenance of records of the firearms and guns, so that they can be traced to their owners in event of crime. Another avowed purpose of registration is to place a ceiling on the number of registered firearms and guns.[46]

NOTES

1. See generally 49 Law & Contem Prob 1 (Winter 1986).
2. See generally 16 UCD L Rev 137 (1982-1983).
3. Note J. Levin, "The Right to Bear Arms: The Development of the American Experience," Chi-Kent L Rev (Fall-Winter 1971) at p. 130.
4. See J. Wright & P. Rossi, Weapons, Crime and Violence in America (Executive Summary) National Institute of Justice (1981) at p. 9.
5. Infra note 1 at p. 223.
6. See "For the Defense" (May 1988), Defense Law News, at p. 6: note 22 Pub Aff Rep (Institute of Governmental Studies, Univ. of California, October 1981) at pp. 1 et seq.
7. See 6 Hamline L Rev (1986) at p. 278.
8. See Ala. Const., art. 1, sec. 26, Alas. Const., art. 1, §19, Ariz. Const., art. 2, §26, Ark. Const., art. 2, §5, Colo. Const., art 2, §13, Conn. Const., art. 1, §15, Fla. Const., art. 1, §8, Ga. Const., §1-802 (copied from the U.S. Const.), Idaho Const., art. 1, §11, Ill. Const., art 1, §22, Ind. Const., art. 1 §32, Kan. Const., bill of rights §4, Ky. Const. bill of rights, §1, La. Const., art 1, §11, Me. Const., art. 1, §16, Mass. Const., part 1, art. 17, Mich. Const., art 1, §6, Miss. Const., art 3, §12, Mo. Const., art. 1, §23, Mont. Const., art. 2, §12, Nev. Const., art. 1, §11, N.H. Const., part 1 (bill of rights), art. 2a, N.M. Const., art. 2, §6, N.Y. const., civil rights §4, N.C. Const., art. 1, §30, Ohio Const., art. 1, §4, Okla. Const., art. 2, §26, Oe. Const., art. 1, §27, Pa. Const., art. 1, §21, R.I. Const., art. 1, §22, S.C. Const., art. 1, §20, S.D. Const., art. 6, §25, Tenn. Const., art. 1, §26, Tex. Const., art. 1, §23, Utah Const., art. 1, §6, Vt. Const., ch. 1, art. 16, Va. Const., art 1, §13, Wash. Const., art 1, §24, Wyo. Const., art. 1, §24.
9. See 6 Hamline L Rev (1986) at p. 278.
10. See generally Kleck & Bordua, "The Factual Foundation for Certain Key Assumptions of Gun Control," 5 Law & Pol Q 271 (1983).
11. Note Cook, "Reducing Injury and Death Rates in Robbery," 6 Policy Analysis 21 (1980).

12. See Cook, "The Role of Firearms in Violent Crime," Criminal Violence 255-257 (1982).

13. See generally 51 Chi-Kent L Rev 62 (1974).

14. See *New York Times* (June 16, 1988) at pp. C1 and C14.

15. Id.

16. Infra note 7 at p. 431.

17. For example, see Galvan v. Superior Court, 452 P2d 930 (Cal., 1969).

18. Ordinance No. 81-11, Village of Morton Grove, An Ordinance Regulating the Possession of Firearms and Other Dangerous Weapons:

WHEREAS, it has been determined that in order to promote and protect the health and safety and welfare of the public it is necessary to regulate the possession of firearms and other dangerous weapons, and

WHEREAS, the Corporate Authorities of the Village of Morton Grove have found and determined that the easy and convenient availability of certain types of firearms and weapons have increased the potentiality of firearm related deaths and injuries, and

WHEREAS, handguns play a major role in the commission of homicide, aggravated assault, and armed robbery, and accidental injury and death.

NOW, THEREFORE, BE IT ORDAINED BY THE PRESIDENT AND BOARD OF TRUSTEES OF THE VILLAGE OF MORTON GROVE, COOK COUNTY, ILLINOIS, AS FOLLOWS:

SECTION 1: The Corporate Authorities do hereby incorporate the foregoing WHEREAS clauses into this Ordinance, thereby making the findings as herein above set forth.

SECTION 2: That Chapter 132 of the Code or Ordinances of the Village of Morton Grove be and is hereby amended by the addition of the following section:

Section 132.102. Weapons Control

(A) *Definitions:*

Firearm: "Firearm" means any device, by whatever name known, which is designed to expel a projectile or projectiles by the action of an explosion, expansion of gas or escape of gas; excluding however:

(1) Any pneumatic gun, spring gun or B-B gun which expels a single globular projectile not exceeding .18 inches in diameter.

(2) Any device used exclusively for signalling or safety and required or recommended by the United States Coast Guard or the Interstate Commerce Commission.

Barrel length of less than 26 inches, or a barrel length of less than 18 inches or any bomb, bomb-shell, grenade, bottle or other container containing an explosive substance of over one-quarter ounce for like purposes, such as, but not limited to black powder bombs and Molotov cocktails or artillery projectiles; or

(3) Any handgun, unless the same has been rendered permanently inoperative.

(C) Subsection B(1) shall not apply to or affect any peace officer.

(D) Subsection B(2) shall not apply to or affect the following:

(1) Peace officers;

(2) Wardens, superintendents and keepers of prisons, penitentiaries, jails and other institutions for the detention of persons accused or convicted of an offense;

(3) Members of the Armed Services or Reserve Forces of the United States or the

Illinois National Guard or the Reserve Officers Training Corps. while in the performance of their official duties;

(4) Transportation of machine guns to those persons authorized under Subparagraphs (1) and (2) of this subsection to possess machine guns, if the machine guns are broken down in a non-functioning state or not immediately accessible.

(E) Subsection B(3) does not apply to or affect the following:

(1) Peace officers or any person summoned by any peace officer to assist in making arrests or preserving the peace while he is actually engaged in assisting such officer and if such handgun was provided by the peace officer;

(2) Wardens, superintendents and keepers of prisons, penitentiaries, jails and other institutions for the detention of persons accused or convicted of an offense;

(3) Members of the Armed Services or Reserve Forces of the United States or the Illinois National Guard or the Reserve Officers Training Corps. while in the performance of their official duties;

(4) Special Agents employed by a railroad or a public utility to perform police functions; guards of armored car companies; watchmen and security guards actually and regularly employed in the commercial or industrial operation for the protection of persons employed and private property related to such commercial or industrial operation;

(5) Agents and investigators of the Illinois Legislative Investigating Commission authorized by the commission to carry such weapons;

(6) Licensed gun collectors;

(7) Licensed gun clubs provided the gun club has premises from which it operates and maintains possession and control of handguns used by its members, and has procedures and facilities for keeping such handguns in a safe place under the control of the club's chief officer, at all times when they are not being used for target shooting or other sporting or recreational purposes at the premises of the gun club; and gun club members while such members are using their handguns at the gun club premises;

(8) A possession of an antique firearm;

(9) Transportation of handguns to those persons authorized under Subparagraph 1 through 8 of this subsection to possess handguns if the handguns are broken down in a non-functioning state or not immediately accessible;

(10) Transportation of handguns by persons from a licensed gun club to another licensed gun club or transportation from a licensed gun club to a gun club outside the limits of Morton Grove; provided however that the transportation is for the purpose of engaging in competitive target shooting or for the purpose of permanently keeping said handgun at such new gun club; and provided further that at all times during such transportation said handgun shall have trigger locks securely fastened to the handgun.

(F) *Penalty:*

(1) Any person violating Section B(1) or B(2) of this Ordinance shall be guilty of a misdemeanor and shall be fined not less than $100.00 nor more than $500.00 or incarcerated for up to six months for each such offense.

(2) Any person violating Section B(3) of this Ordinance shall be guilty of a petty offense and shall be fined no less than $50.00 nor more than $500.00 for such offense. Any person violating Section B(3) of this Ordinance more than one time shall be guilty of a misdemeanor and shall be fined no less than $100.00 nor more than $500.00 or incarcerated for up to six months for each such offense.

(3) Upon conviction of a violation of Section B(1) through B(3) of this Ordinance, any weapon seized shall be confiscated by the trial court and when no longer needed for evidentiary purposes, the court may transfer such weapon to the Morton Grove Police Dept. who shall destroy them.

(G) *Voluntary Delivery to Police Department:*

(1) If a person voluntarily and peaceably delivers and abandons to the Morton Grove Police Dept. any weapon mentioned in Sections B(1) through B(3), such delivery shall preclude the arrest and prosecution of such person on a charge of violating any provision of this Ordinance with respect to the weapon voluntarily delivered. Delivery under this section may be made at the headquarters of the police department or by summoning a police officer to the person's residence or place of business. Every weapon to be delivered and abandoned to the police department under this paragraph shall be unloaded and securely wrapped in a package and in the case of delivery to the police headquarters, the package shall be carried in open view. No person who delivers and abandons a weapon under this section shall be required to furnish identification, photographs or fingerprints. No amount of money shall be paid for any weapon delivered or abandoned under this paragraph.

(2) Whenever any weapon is surrendered under this section, the police department shall inquire of all law enforcement agencies whether such weapon is needed as evidence and if the same is not needed as evidence, it shall be destroyed.

(H) All weapons ordered confiscated by the court under the provisions of Section F(3) and all weapons received by the Morton Grove Police Department under and by virtue of Section G shall be held and identified as to owner, where possible, by the Morton Grove Police Department for a period of five years prior to their being destroyed.

(I) *Construction:*

Nothing in this Ordinance shall be construed or applied to necessarily require or excuse non compliance with a provision of the laws of the State of Illinois or of the laws of the United States. This Ordinance and the penalties proscribed for violation hereof, shall not supersede, but shall supplement all statutes of the State of Illinois or of the United States in which similar conduct may be prohibited or regulated.

(J) *Severability:*

If any provisions of this Ordinance or the application thereof to any person or circumstance is held invalid, the remainder of this Ordinance and the applicability of such provision to other persons not similarly situated or to other circumstances shall not be affected thereby.

(K) the provisions of this Ordinance shall take effect ninety (90) days from and after its passage, approval, and publication in pamphlet form acording to law.

SECTION 3: That this Ordinance shall be published in pamphlet form. Said pamphlet shall be received as evidence of the passage and legal publication of this Ordinance.

19. See Quilici v. Village of Morton Grove, 532 F Supp 1169 (N.D. Ill., 1981), aff 695 F2d 261 (7th Cir., 1982) cert den 104 S Ct 194 (1983).

20. See Doe v. City and County of San Francisco, 186 Cal Rptr 380 (Cal. App., 1982).

21. Note McIntosh v. Washington, 395 A2d 744 (D.C., 1978).

22. See 13 St. Marys L J 601 (1982).

23. D.C. Code Ann. Sec. 6.2301 (1981); also infra note 7 at p. 427.

24. Note Wright, "Public Opinion and Gun Control: A Comparison of Results from Two Recent National Surveys," 455 Annals 24 (1981).

25. See New York Times (May 24, 1988) at p. D27.

26. See Hartford Courant (May 24, 1988) at p. A2 and (June 15, 1988), at p. C2.

27. Note the Preamble to Proposition 15 (1982 Cal. Adv. Legis. Serv., 1114):

> (5) The people of the state of California understand the fears of many voters that gun control laws, while beginning with registration, some day will end with confiscation. By enacting this initiative, the people of the state of California can for the first time guarantee that this fear cannot come true. The people of the state of California here forbid their elected representatives in the Legislature from ever passing any laws to take registered handguns away from law-abiding citizens. The people do not intend that this initiative will be a first step toward any confiscatory gun control legislation. (6) The people of the state of California recognize that most firearms are long rifles and shotguns, which have many lawful uses in such recreational sports as hunting, and in self-protection as well. By enacting this initiative, law-abiding people are guaranteed the right to own and purchase long rifles and shotguns without limitation. Through this initiative, the people attempt only to put reasonable regulations on concealable handguns and to prevent their use in the commission of crimes.

28. See 49 Law & Contem Prob 1 (Winter 1986) at p. 221.

29. See Sax, "Takings and the Police Power," 74 Yale L J 36 (1964).

30. Infra note 28 at p. 225.

31. Pennsylvania Coal Co. v. Mahon, 260 US 393 (1922) at p. 413. Justice Brandeis's dissent therein expressed a dissimilar view: "Every restriction upon the use of property imposed in the exercise of the police power deprives the owner of some right theretofore enjoyed, and is, in that sense an abridgement by the State of the rights in property" (at p. 417).

32. Infra note 28 at pp. 226 et seq.

33. 344 US 149 (1952).

34. Id. at p. 153.

35. See Fesjian v. Jefferson, 399 A2d 861 (D.C. 1979) and Samuels v. McCurdy, 267 US 188 (1925).

36. Infra note 28 at p. 233:

> *Noxious Use*. Police power also includes the state's power to abate a nuisance, that is, to forbid the "noxious use" of property. Therefore, some cases have held that if a state confiscates or orders the destruction of a noxious use, it is necessarily using its police power and need not compensate. For example, in *Lawton v. Steel*,[64] the Supreme Court upheld a New York statute that stated that any fishing net maintained in the water in violation of the fishing laws "is hereby declared to be, and is, a public nuisance, and may be abated and summarily destroyed by any person."[65] After asserting that the preservation of game and fish was within the proper domain of the police power,[66] the

Court found the summary abatement, without the fifth amendment protections of due process and just compensation, to be legitimate.[67] In *Adams v. Milwaukee*,[68] the destruction of potentially unwholesome milk was found to be the abatement of a public nuisance, and the owners of the milk were not compensated. Similarly, in *North American Cold Storage Co. v. Chicago*,[69] the Court held that unwholesome food "should be summarily seized and destroyed to prevent the danger which would come from eating it."[70]

64. 152. U.S. 133 (1894).
65. Id. at 135.
66. Id. at 138.
67. Id. at 140.
68. 228 U.S. 572, 584 (1913).
69. 211 U.S. 306 (1908).
70. Id. at 315.

37. See D. Bayley, Forces of order: Police behavior in Japan and the United States 160 (1979):

It is clearly unrealistic to expect any police force to disarm if the populace at large is allowed to possess substantial quantities of firearms. At the same time, willingness of the police to use firearms may affect the way guns are viewed by society. Specifically, the fact that police accept the inevitability of armed confrontations with offenders may reduce pressure for more stringent gun control laws. Consider, for instance, what would happen if American police officials publicly announced their commitment to strict gun control legislation and then announced they would disarm themselves as an example of how safe society is most of the time. The immediate reaction, of course, would be astonishment and incredulity. The long run effect would be to make the killing of policemen wanton acts. If policemen were unarmed and then killed, the implicit norms of fairness would be violated. They wouldn't have a chance. The public would have a greater difficulty than now in denying responsibility for protecting police officers. Support for strict enforcement of penalties against guns in crime would stiffen, as would pressure for hand gun control legislation. Guns in police hands and guns in private hands are related. But there is more symmetry in the relationship than is usually recognized. The police will feed compelled to be armed as long as much of the populace is. But the populace may not limit arms ownership without persistent encouragement from the police, especially willingness to sacrifice some of the appearance of self reliance. The police probably possess more initiative than they are willing to exercise.

38. (See also Appendix).

FIREARMS LICENSES ISSUED, DENIED AND REVOKED

Fiscal year	Licenses issued	Percent	Licenses denied	Percent	Licenses revoked	Percent	Total action	Total (percent)
1969	77,573	97.85	1,705	2.15	0	0	79.278	100
1970	138,865	98.22	2,512	1.78	8	.006	141,385	100
1971	144,548	99.29	1,032	.71	7	.005	145,587	100
1972	147,026	98.34	1,683	1.13	42	.03	148,751	100
1973	148,600	98.88	1,669	1.11	12	.008	150,281	100
1974	156,443	99.01	1,540	.97	17	.011	158,281	100
1975	161,927	99.74	423	.26	7	.004	162,357	100
1976	165,697	99.71	470	.28	6	.004	166,173	100
Transition quarter	40,803	99.58	172	.42	1	.002	40,976	100
1977	173,484	99.75	423	.24	10	.006	173,917	100
1978	166,698	99.81	319	.19	0	0	167,017	100
Total	1,521,664	99.21	11,948	.78	100	.007	1,533,722	100

39. See A. Gottlieb, The Rights of Gun Owners (1981) at pp. 82-142.

40. —NYS2d—(Westchester County, May 19, 1988).

41. "Although Respondent raises peripheral questions concerning his underlying conduct which led to the arrest for petit larceny and the supposed promise of a favorable disposition in exchange for his admission, the key issue is whether his guilty plea to the violation of trespass nearly 2½ years ago, by itself, renders him unfit to possess a pistol license. The Court believes that such a plea does not render Respondent unfit. Without more, the County Attorney's Office cannot succeed on this application."

42. Infra note 7 at pp. 420-421.

43. Wash Rev. Code Ann., Section 9.41.070 (1983-1984).

42. Section 400 et seq. of New York Penal Law.

45. See Section 2C:58-3 of N.J. Stat. Ann. (1982) and Mass. Gen. Law Ann., ch. 140, Section 129B (1982).

46. On the broad issue of judicial review, see Burton v. Sills, 248 A2d 521 (N.J. 1968), app dism 394 US 812 (1969).

2

Terminology and Meaning of the Second Amendment

2.1 INTRODUCTION

> "A well-regulated militia being necessary to the security of a free state, the right of the people to keep and bear Arms shall not be infringed."
>
> *Second Amendment to U.S. Constitution*

These twenty-seven words of the Second Amendment to the U.S. Constitution, the veritable Bible of the National Rifle Association of America and its millions of gun-toting members,[1] have been the subject of intense controversy for more than 200 years. It was James Madison to whom the first Congress delegated the task of drafting a Bill of Rights, and this gifted patriot (and later fourth president of the United States) proposed, among other rights, that "the right of the people to keep and bear arms shall not be infringed; a well armed and well regulated militia being the best security of a free country; but no person religiously scrupulous of bearing arms shall be compelled to render military service in person."[2] Madison's proposal was modified in the House of Representatives so that the "militia clause" came before the proposed recognition of the right to keep and bear arms; the third clause on conscientious objectors was deleted. Both the House and the U.S. Senate immediately passed the revised proposal without further modification.

It took the U.S. Supreme Court almost a hundred years to pronounce its first decision on the Second Amendment. In the year 1876 in United States v. Cruikshank,[3] the highest court found that the right to keep and bear arms was not a right guaranteed by the Constitution, was not dependent on the Constitution for its existence, was protected only against infringement by the federal government, and in any case its application to personal rights was only in the context of the freedom of the states to have their own militias.[4] In effect, the right of the individual was given constitutional protection only to the extent that the right of the particular individual to have a gun was essential to the ability of the state to have an effective militia. It would be inane to accept the view that an armed citizenry of men and women using guns could take up the armed cudgel purely for their individual political whim and political fancy. Only anarchy would result, and the Preamble to the U.S. Constitution—"to insure domestic tranquility, provide for the common defense, and promote the general welfare"—would be placed in serious jeopardy. The National Rifle Association of America, however, takes the position that "law-abiding Americans are constitutionally entitled to legal ownership and use of firearms." Yet the general counsel of that organization admits that the right to keep and bear arms "was not created by the Second Amendment; rather, this basic individual right developed in England before this continent was colonized, predated the constitution, and was part of the common law heritage of the thirteen original colonies."[5] Indeed, the possession of guns under English common law was never an absolute right; at most it was a "privilege" to keep and bear arms. Similarly, during the American Revolution, the so-called right to keep and bear arms was designed to prevent the newly formed federal government from destroying state militias. The "right" was a collective or corporate right, not an individual right, to insure that the balance between liberty and authority, within the newly formed union, would be maintained. Personal protection or self-defense was not the issue as Roscoe Pound said: "In the urban industrial society of today a general right to bear efficient arms so as to be enabled to resist oppression by the government would mean that gangs could exercise an extra-legal rule which could defeat the whole Bill of Rights."[6]

The *New York Times* (July 21, 1987 at A18) reported that John M. Snyder "the chief lobbyist for the Citizens Committee for the Right to Keep and Bear Arms," had written to the Cardinal Prefect of the Sacred

Congregation for the Causes of Saints in Rome, Italy, "requesting that Gabriel Possenti be designated a saint."

Mr. Snyder bases his case on an incident in which Gabriel Possenti, a priest who lived in Italy from 1838 to 1862 and was reputedly a fine marksman in his youth, is said to have put to rout a squad of renegade soldiers with a brace of pistols.

He took one pistol from a startled soldier, then used it to commandeer another from a second soldier. When their leader, a sergeant, sneered, the priest took aim at a lizard in the road and drilled it dead with a single shot. Impressed, the soldiers took to their heels.

Designating the priest the Patron of Handgunners, Mr. Snyder asserted in his letter, would show that "an instrument, in the hands of a person committed in heart, mind and soul to Almighty God, may be used to bring about practical good here on earth."

2.2 "A WELL-REGULATED MILITIA"

The Second Amendment begins with the words "a well-regulated militia," and advocates of the right to keep and bear arms interpret the word "militia" to be an "unorganized militia," in the sense that the populace at large, or at least members of the populace capable of bearing arms, have a right to keep and bear arms. This "right" is advocated as a check against any excesses of any and all government. However, this extreme view is not supported by history, for the framers of the Constitution had no need to create a "right to revolution" against the excesses of any and all government nor a license to band together in paramilitary organizations; the checks and balances system within the Constitution itself precluded excesses of any and all government. Also, "well-regulated," the adjective modifying "militia," is the very antithesis of "unorganized" (modifying "militia"), which advocates of the right to keep and bear arms contend give the populace at large the right to keep and bear arms. Indeed, "a well-regulated militia" is not an "unorganized militia"; the thrust of the Second Amendment was to guard against federal attempts to disarm or abolish *organized* state militias.[7]

The militia system during precolonial times in the United States was a carryover from the English practice, whereby every adult male was required to keep and bear his own arms, for there were no police and no standing army in peacetime.[8] Keeping and bearing arms was a duty of each male adult for purposes of law enforcement as well as for military service.[9] Georgia actually required by a 1770 statute that every "male white person" carry a rifle or pistol every time he attended church, and church officials were empowered to search each parishoner no less than 14 times per year to assure compliance.[10] The First Militia Act of 1792 defined the militia as a formal military force of the entire able- bodied military-age male citizenry of the United States and required those males to own their own firearms.[11] The *formal* nature of "militia" was substantiated almost 200 years later in United States v. Oakes, when the Tenth U.S. Court of Appeals declared that the Second Amendment did not guarantee an individual the right to keep an unregistered firearm, since the firearm had no connection with the militia.[12] Similarly, in 1982 a federal district court in Texas enjoined private military activities because the Second Amendment delineated the keeping and bearing of arms only for a well-regulated militia organized by the state of Texas.[13] Today the state militia or National Guard is given formal training in the use of weapons issued by the federal government; these weapons are unsuited for private possession, and the U.S. Supreme Court has held that states may not control nor authorize arms in a manner that would conflict with the federal government's use of state militia for national defense.[14] Formal state militia described in the Second Amendment was the vehicle to prevent the establishment of a standing federal army that could oppress the states and the citizens thereof.[15] Under Article I, Section 8, of the Constitution the federal government may call forth the militia for purposes of combatting invasion and insurrection or for executing the laws of the Union.[16]

"A well-regulated militia" clearly negates any individual right to keep and bear arms. The Kansas Supreme Court in 1905 in Salina v. Blaksley expressly held that only the people, not the individual, have a right to keep and bear arms, a collective right guaranteed by Section 4 of Kansas's constitutional bill of rights, which provides that "the people have the right to bear arms for their defense and security."[17] The highest Kansas court declared that this provision only "refers to the people as a collective body."

Most recently, in Sandidge v. United States[18] the appellant who was convicted of carrying a pistol without a license endeavored to argue that the District of Columbia firearms statute under which he was convicted violated his constitutional right to "keep and bear arms."[19] The court sermonized as follows:

We agree with numerous other courts that "the Second Amendment guarantees a collective rather than an individual right." United States v. Warin, 530 F.2d 103, 106 (6th Cir.), cert. denied, 426 U.S. 948 (1976); accord Stevens v. United States, 440 F.2d 144, 149 (6th Cir. 1971); United States v. Kozerski, 518 F.Supp. 1082, 1090 (D.N.H. 1981), aff'd mem., 740 F.2d 952 (1st Cir.), cert. denied, 469 U.S. 842 (1984); Annot. 37 A.L.R. Fed. 696, 706 (1978) (citing cases). That is to say, it protects a state's right to raise and regulate a militia by prohibiting Congress from enacting legislation that will interfere with that right. The second amendment says nothing that would prohibit a state (or the legislature for the District of Columbia) from restricting the use or possession of weapons in derogation of the government's own right to enroll a body of militiamen "bearing arms supplied by themselves" as in bygone days. United States v. Miller, 307 U.S. 174, 179 (1939). In sum, "[t]he right to keep and bear arms is not a right conferred upon the people by the federal constitution. Whatever rights the people may have depend upon local legislation. . . . " Cases v. United States, 131 F.2d 916, 921 (1st Cir. 1942), cert. denied, 319 U.S. 770 (1943).

Appellant's reliance on United States v. Miller, 307 U.S. 174 (1939), is misplaced. In Miller, the Supreme Court held that the National Firearms Act of 1934 did not violate the second amendment:

In the absence of any evidence tending to show that possession or use of a "shotgun having a barrel of less than eighteen inches in length" at this time has some reasonable relationship to the preservation or efficiency of a well regulated militia, we cannot say that the Second Amendment guarantees the right to keep and bear such an instrument.

307 U.S. at 178. We reject appellant's contention that Miller stands for the proposition that Congress may regulate only those classes of weapons which have no relationship to the militia. The Supreme Court "did not intend to formulate a general rule in Miller, but merely dealt with the facts of that case." Warin, 530 F.2d at 106 (citing Cases, 131 F.2d at 922). Given the destructive capabilities of modern weaponry, it is inconceivable and irrational to suggest, as the logic of appellant's argument does, that Congress may only regulate weapons which have no possible relationship to the common defense today "such as a flintlock musket or a matchlock harquebus." n2 Id.

The purpose of the second amendment is "to preserve the effectiveness and assure the continuation of the state militia." United States v. Oakes, 564 F.2d 384, 387 (10th Cir. 1977), cert. denied, 435 U.S. 926 (1978). Appellant cannot show that possession of a handgun by an individual bears any relationship to the District of Columbia's desire and ability to preserve a well regulated militia. See D.C. Code arts. 39-106, -201 (1981) (provides for organized militia, called the National Guard, to be armed by government); Miller, 307 U.S. at 178;

Warin, 530 F.2d at 106 (possession of submachine gun by individual has no relationship to preservation or efficiency of a well regulated militia).[20]

n2 Appellant's argument that the second amendment guarantees an individual the right to bear only those weapons that one person can operate does not supply a meaningful limitation. That interpretation would still put lethal weapons such as high powered rifles, machine guns, and even some antitank weapons beyond the scope of legislative control. See Cannon Control, Washington Post, Dec. 19, 1986, at A20, col. 1. It is inconceivable that the Supreme Court intended in Miller to recognize the right of unrestricted access to such weapons.

The kind of the weapon was the subject of Crowley Cultery Co. v. United States where the federal district court in Illinois was called upon to examine the Switchblade Knife Act as to its constitutionality, inter alia, under the Second Amendment. As the court explained its finding of constitutionality, "federal statutes barring or regulating weapons have withstood various constitutional challenges. See, e.g., United States v. Lauchli, 444 F.2d 1037 (7th Cir. 1971) (National Firearms Act and Gun Control Act do not violate Second Amendment; prosecution brought for violation of Act not violative of defendant's Fifth Amendment privilege against self-incrimination); United States v. Warin, 530 F.2d 103 (6th Cir. 1976) (provisions of National Firearms Act and Gun Control Act prohibiting possession of unregistered machine gun do not violate Second or Ninth Amendments).

Many states, including Illinois, Indiana and Wisconsin, similarly make the manufacture, sale or possession of switchblade knives criminal offenses. Ill. Rev. Stat. ch. 38, par. 24-1(a) (1) (1985); Ind. Code Ann. sec. 35-47-5-2 (Burns 1985); Wisc. Stat. Ann. sec. 941.24 (West 1982). In an early case, State v. Workman, 35 W. Va. 367, 14 S.E. 9 (1891), the constitutionality of a state statute prohibiting the carrying of a concealed weapon was upheld. The defendant argued, among other things, that the state law violated the Second Amendment. The Supreme Court of West Virginia pointed out that "to regulate a conceded right (the right to bear arms) is not necessarily to infringe the same." 14 S.E. at 11. The court found the statutes to be a valid regulation of the right and therefore not violative of the Second Amendment. In reaching its decision, the court examined the framers' intent and the purpose of the Amendment and observed:

. . . in regard to the kind of arms referred to in the amendment, it must be held to refer to the weapons of warfare to be used by the militia, such as swords, guns, rifles and muskets,—arms to be used in defending the state and civil liberty,—and not to pistols, bowie-knives, brass knuckles, billies, and such other weapons as are usually employed in brawls, street fights, duels, and affrays, and are only habitually carried by bullies, blackguards and desperadoes, to the terror of the community and the injury of the state. Bish. Crim. St. sec. 792.

More recently, Masters v. State, 653 S.W.2d 944 (Tex. Ct. App. 1983), aff'd., 685 S.W.2d 654 (Tex. Crim. App. 1985), held that defendant's conviction for carrying two sword-like weapons in violation of state law did not deny defendant any right guaranteed him by the Second Amendment.

2.3 "NECESSARY FOR THE SECURITY OF A FREE STATE"

The second phrase of the Second Amendment, "necessary for the security of a free state," speaks in terms of the importance of that "well-regulated militia," which is vital and necessary for the security of a state that desires to remain free. Deterrence of oppression is the key to understanding why the "right" to keep and bear arms is a collective or corporate "right" and not an individual "right," for no single individual can constitute the "well-regulated militia" which is "necessary for the security of a free state." Even James Madison proposed that "the right of the *people* to keep and bear arms shall not be infringed; a well-armed and well-regulated militia being the best security of a free country."[21] On the other hand, it is argued that in the Second Amendment the phrase "for the common defense" was deliberately rejected as a modifier of "the right to keep and bear arms," thereby contending that the purpose of the Second Amendment was not to provide for security and defense.[22] The counterpoint of the same argument is that the right to keep and bear arms belongs to the individual, consonant with the natural right of self-defense at common law. As the Georgia court in 1846 stated, "self-defense, therefore, as it is justly called the primary law of nature, so it is not, neither can it be in fact, taken away by the law of society."[23] Thus, advocates of arms possession by individuals justify their conclusion by the uniquely American frontier experience of yesterday. Today, however, there is no such frontier, and people no longer depend upon guns for day-to-day survival.[24]

2.4 "THE RIGHT OF THE PEOPLE"

The third phrase, "the right of the people," admittedly refers to something more than an entitlement that exists only because it is recognized and therefore can be taken away through democratic law-making processes. A "right" cannot be eliminated through democratic law-making processes, although that ''right'' can be qualified by reference to reasonableness, as illustrated by the Fourth Amendment, which balances the ''right of the people to be secure in their persons, houses, papers and effects'' against ''unreasonable searches and seizures.'' The Second Amendment also balances the ''right of the people'' in the sense that collective action and not individual action is necessary to protect it.[25] Thus, the entitlement is at most a ''privilege'' to keep and bear arms.

''People,'' as found in both the Second and Ninth Amendments, means ''states'' or collections of persons.[26] The fact that the Tenth Amendment distinguishes between ''people'' and ''state'' does not detract from the obvious conclusion that the term ''people'' connotes more than the individual. This collective-right view does not mean that the ''right of the people'' can be construed in the Second Amendment as something less than ''people'' or collectiveness.[27] The term ''people'' includes individuals, but that does not mean that all individuals have a right to keep and bear arms; infants, idiots, lunatics, and felons, among others, are obviously excluded.[28]

2.5 "TO KEEP AND BEAR ARMS"

The fourth phrase of the Second Amendment, ''to keep and bear arms,'' is admittedly controversial because of its ambiguity. For example, the militia ''bear'' arms, while civilians ''carry'' arms, thereby restricting the ''right'' to members of the militia.[29] Also, the militia ''keep'' arms in that the arms are not private property but belong to the governments; an individual, not a member of the militia, would ''possess'' arms, at most.

''Arms'' delineated under the Second Amendment must refer to weapons used by militia, and therefore would probably exclude hunting knives, muskets and rifles, hatchets, swords, billy clubs, and other weapons or guns that individuals rely on for pleasure and for hunting, activities that are the very backbone of the National Rifle Association of America and its millions of members. The U.S. Supreme Court in its 1939 decision in United States v. Miller rejected the military character of a ''shotgun having a barrel of less than 18 inches in length'' because the shotgun has no ''reasonable relationship to the preservation or efficiency of a well regulated militia.''[30] But the prime query is not necessarily the nature of the ''arms''; it is whether or not the defendant was a weapon holder acting in the role of a member of the militia. [In

Cases v. United States the First U.S. Court of Appeals in 1942 rejected the idea that individuals were part of the militia versus nonmilitia weapons dichotomy.[31]] In 1972 Justice William O. Douglas in Adams v. Williams[32] took occasion to remark that "there is no reason why all pistols should not be barred to everyone except the police. . . . Our decisions belie the argument (of watering down the Second Amendment), for the Second Amendment, as noted, was designed to keep alive the militia."[33] One writer in 1983 erroneously contends that the constitutional protection under the Second Amendment extends only to weapons which are "of the kind in common use among law-abiding people today, useful and appropriate not just for military purposes but also for law enforcement and individual self-defense, and linearly descended from the kinds of weapons known to the Founders."[34] His delineation of weapons is mere wishful thinking and unsupportable in history and in constitutional law; undoubtedly his principal purpose was to erect a barrier to state and local regulation of gun ownership, as illustrated in Quilici v. Village of Morton Grove, where the local community in Illinois enacted an ordinance banning the private ownership of handguns.[35] The Oregon Supreme Court in 1980, however, took a broad view of "arms," a term "used by the drafters of the constitutions" was

> probably . . . intended to include those weapons used by settlers for both personal and military defense. The term 'arms' was not limited to firearms, but included several handcarried weapons commonly used for defense. The term 'arms' would not have included cannon or other heavy ordnance not kept by militiamen. . . . Advanced weapons of modern warfare have never been intended for personal possession and protection. . . . If the text and purpose of the constitutional guarantee relied exclusively on the preference for a militia, then the terms 'arms' most likely would include only the modern day equivalents of the weapons used by colonial militiamen."[36]

2.6 "SHALL NOT BE INFRINGED"

The final or closing phrase of the Second Amendment favors neither the collective nor the individual right interpretation, although the language "shall not be infringed" appears to be a stronger admonition than "Congress shall make no law."[37] "The term "infringe" means to defeat, to frustrate, to violate, to destroy, to hinder,[38] and sends out signals to legislation of Congress, to state, local, and federal activities, and to the private conduct of citizens that the "right" guaranteed by the Second Amendment must stand.[39]

2.7 STATE CONSTITUTIONAL PROVISIONS

Of the fifty states in the Union only thirteen have no constitutional provision that tracks or elaborates upon the Second Amendment on the right to keep and bear arms. They are California, Delaware, Iowa, Maryland, Minnesota, Nebraska, Nevada, New Hampshire, New Jersey, New York, North Dakota, West Virginia, and Wisconsin.[40] The majority of thirty-seven states with constitutional provisions modeled after the Second Amendment runs the gamut of the argument as to individual versus collective right. Those states holding to the individual right theory in their constitutions include Alabama (every citizen has a right to bear arms in defense of himself and the state[41]), Arizona (the right of the individual citizen to bear arms in defense of himself or the state shall not be impaired, but nothing in this section shall be construed as authorizing individuals or corporations to organize, maintain, or employ an armed body of men[42]), Colorado (the right of no person to keep and bear arms in defense of his home, person, and property, or in aid of the civil power when legally summoned, shall be called in question, but nothing herein contained shall be construed to justify the practice of carrying concealed weapons[43]), Connecticut (a citizen has a fundamental right to bear arms in self-defense, which must be protected by procedural due process[44]), Illinois (the right of the individual citizen to keep and bear arms shall not be infringed, subject only to the police power[45]), Louisiana (the right of each citizen to keep and bear arms shall not be abridged, but this provision shall not prevent the passage of laws to prohibit the carrying of weapons concealed on the person[46]), Maine (every citizen has the right to keep and bear arms for the common defense, and this right shall never be questioned[47]), Michigan (every person has a right to keep and bear arms for the defense of himself and the state[48]), Mississippi (the right of every citizen to keep and bear arms in defense of his home, person, or property, or in aid of the civil power where thereto legally summoned, shall not be called into question, but the legislature may regulate or forbid carrying concealed weapons[49]), Missouri (the right of every citizen to keep and bear arms in defense of his person, home and property, or when lawfully summoned in aid of the civil power, shall not be questioned, but this shall not justify the wearing of concealed weapons[50]), Montana (the right of every person to keep or bear arms in defense of his own home, person or property, or in aid of the civil power when thereto legally summoned, shall not be called in question, but nothing herein contained shall be held to permit the carrying of concealed weapons[51]), New Mexico (no law shall abridge the right of the citizen to keep and bear arms for security and defense, for lawful hunting and recreational use and for other lawful purposes, but nothing herein shall be held to permit the carrying of concealed weapons[52]), Oklahoma (the right of a citizen to keep and bear arms in defense of his home, person, or property, or in aid of the civil power when thereunto legally summoned, shall never be prohibited, but nothing herein contained shall prevent the legislature from regulating the carrying of weapons[53]), Texas (every citizen shall have the right to keep and bear arms in the lawful defense of himself or the state, but the legislature shall have the power by law to regulate the wearing of arms with a view to prevent crime[54]), and Washington, (the right of the individual citizen to bear arms in defense of himself or the state shall not be impaired, but nothing in this section shall be construed as authorizing individuals or corporations to organize, maintain, or employ an armed body of men[55]). Thus, fifteen states adhere to what may be described as the individual right theory under the Second Amendment.

In sharp contrast are those twenty-two states holding to the collective right theory: Alaska (a well-regulated militia being necessary to the security of a free state, the right of the people to keep and bear arms shall not be infringed[56]), Arkansas (the citizens of this state shall have the right to keep and bear arms for their common defense[57]), Florida (the right of the people to keep and bear arms in defense of themselves and of the lawful authority of the state shall not be infringed, except that the manner of bearing arms may be regulated by law[58]), Georgia (the right of the people to keep and bear arms shall not be infringed, but the General Assembly shall have the power to prescribe the manner in which arms may be borne[59]), Hawaii (a well-regulated militia being necessary to the security of a free state, the right of the people to keep and bear arms shall not be infringed[60]), Idaho (the people have the right to keep and bear arms, which shall not be abridged, but this provision shall not prevent the passage of laws to govern the carrying of weapons concealed on the person nor prevent passage of legislation providing minimum sentences for crimes committed while in possession of a firearm, nor prevent the passage of legislation providing penalties for the possession of firearms by a convicted felon, nor prevent the passage of any legislation punishing the use of a firearm[61]), Indiana (the people shall have a right to bear arms for the defense of themselves and the state[62]), Kansas (the people have the right to bear arms for their defense and security, but standing armies in time of peace are dangerous to liberty and shall not be tolerated and the military shall be in strict subordination to the civil power[63]), Kentucky (the right to bear arms in defense of themselves and of the state, subject to the power of the General Assembly to enact laws to prevent persons from carrying concealed weapons, is an inherent and inalienable right[64]), Massachusetts (the people have a right to keep and bear arms for the common defense, and in times of peace armies are dangerous to liberty and ought not to be maintained without the consent of the legislature, and the military power shall always be held in exact subordination to the civil authority and be governed by it[65]), North Carolina (a well-regulated militia being necessary to the security of a free state, the right of the people to keep and bear arms shall not be infringed. . . . nothing herein shall justify the practice of carrying concealed weapons or prevent the General Assembly from enacting penal statutes against that practice[66]), Ohio (the people have the right to bear arms for their defense and security, but standing armies in time of peace are dangerous to liberty and shall not be kept, and the military shall be in strict subordination to the civil power[67]), Oregon (the people shall have the right to bear arms for the defense of themselves and the state, but the military shall be kept in strict subordination to the civil power[68]), Pennsylvania (the right of the citizens to bear arms in defense of themselves and the state shall not be questioned[69]), Rhode Island (the right of the people to keep and bear arms shall not be infringed[70]), South Carolina (a well-regulated militia being necessary to the security of a free state, the right of the people to keep and bear arms shall not be infringed[71]), South Dakota (the right of citizens to bear arms in defense of themselves and the state shall not be denied[72]), Tennessee (the citizens of this state have a right to keep and bear arms for their common defense, but the legislature shall have the power by law to regulate the wearing of arms with a view to prevent crime[73]), Utah (the people have the right to bear arms for their security and defense but the legislature may regulate the exercise of this right by law[74]), Vermont (the people have a right to bear arms for the defense of themselves and the state[75]), Virginia (a well-regulated militia composed of the body of the people trained to arms is the proper, natural, and safe defense of a free state; therefore, the right of the people to keep and bear arms shall not be infringed[76]), and Wyoming (the right of citizens to bear arms in defense of themselves and of the state shall not be denied[77]).

A review of these constitutional provisions indicates that a majority of twenty-two states favor the collective right theory under the Second Amendment. The language of the Second Amendment is found almost verbatim in the constitutions of Alaska, Hawaii, North Carolina, South Carolina, and Virginia, although the Virginia constitutional provision is more elaborate. Many state constitutions fail to use both "keep" and "bear" arms, as illustrated in the state constitutions of fourteen states: Alabama, Arizona, Connecticut, Indiana, Kansas, Kentucky, Ohio, Oregon, Pennsylvania, South Dakota, Utah, Vermont, Washington, and Wyoming. This deliberate omission of the word "keep" may be construed to reveal that a great number of states simply did not want to tolerate the "possession" of firearms by individuals. The constitutions of Alabama, Arizona, Connecticut, and Washington, in particular, which otherwise favored the individual right theory, had decided reservations about allowing individuals to "possess" firearms, although in theory at least those individuals could "bear" or carry arms. The motives set forth in the various state constitutional provisions vary from common defense to self-defense, and the "right" itself in some states cannot be infringed or denied or questioned or impaired or ever prohibited, thus raising additional questions as to the power of the legislatures to modify, augment, or delete that constitutional provision. Many states have provisions about concealed weapons, and a number of states include provisions that standing armies are not to be tolerated and that the military establishment must at all times be under exact or strict subordination to the civil power. All in all, the various state constitutional provisions are not clear, precise, and unambiguous in the face of efforts by advocates of gun control to pass meaningful state legislation, as discussed in Chapter 6.

In Alexander v. State of Florida the appellant-defendant was charged with carrying a concealed weapon in violation of state law.[78] His defense was based, among other things, on the Second Amendment, which the court astutely observed made his defense "not a run-of-the mill case," since the National Rifle Association "has submitted an amicus brief." The court proclaimed:

While Americans continue to kill and maim themselves to such an extent that communities may not have a baseball team but they have a SWAT team, English constables still walk their beats without weapons. Most contemporary constitutional scholars agree that the Second Amendment to the United States Constitution concerns only the militia and does not guarantee individuals an unbridled right to carry arms. The Florida Constitution, however, at article 1, section 8, expressly states the right of the people to keep and bear arms in defense of themselves, as well as of the lawful authority of the state, subject to the legislature's authority to regulate the manner of bearing arms. This provision of the Florida Constitution and similar provisions in the constitutions of some thirteen other states have been read as guarantees to individuals, not the people collectively. Sections 776.012 and .031, and 782,02, Florida Statutes, reinforce this view by making it lawful to use firearms in defense of life, home and property, as does the policy declaration in the statute with which we are here most concerned, section 790.25. It would be a futile digression to point out that an alarming percentage of all deaths by firearms are perpetrated by the bearers of arms on acquaintances, friends, family members and themselves.

The purpose of present legislated restrictions on ownership, possession and use of firearms and other weapons is to promote firearms safety and to curb and prevent the use of firearms and other weapons in crime and by incompetent persons without prohibiting their lawful use in defense of life, home or property, by state and federal military, and in other lawful uses such as target practice, marksmanship, and hunting, as permitted by law. Section 790.25(1).[79]

The Florida court affirmed the conviction of the defendant, after pointing out,

In the present case the defense in its sworn motion to dismiss averred that the firearm was in a zippered gun case, and therefore Alexander's carrying of it in his automobile was not in violation of the statute. The state, in its sworn traverse specifically denied that the firearm was in a zippered gun case, stating rather that the firearm was in a man's black leather hand purse. It fortified this with the fact that in another zippered compartment of the same purse the officer found the defendant's wallet, driver's license and various other forms of identification.

What is a zippered gun case? The NRA, in its amicus brief, argues that Alexander's pouch qualifies as a zippered gun case, referring to a catalog that apparently enjoys considerable circulation to show that zippered gun cases may have room for carrying objects additional to the gun. The court looked at the pictures of Alexander's pouch, which are included in an envelope in the record, and determined the pouch was neither a zippered gun case nor a container requiring a top or lid to be opened to make the contents accessible.

In the New York case of Moore v. Gallup the court also took occasion to sound off on the Second Amendment:

> The Second Amendment created no right to bear arms, a right which long antedated the adoption of the Federal Constitution, having originated in a design to strengthen the national militia, an institution first established by King Alfred. (Robertson v. Baldwin, 165 U.S. 275, 281; United States v. Miller, 307 U.S. 174, 179.) Indeed, the main purpose of the Second Amendment was to enable the Federal Government to maintain the public security. (Presser v. Illinois, supra.) Again, the Supreme Court of the United States has held that the right to keep and bear arms is not infringed by laws prohibiting the carrying of concealed weapons (Robertson v. Baldwin, 165 U.S. 275, 281, 282), and Judge Cooley has observed: "The arms intended by the Constitution are such as are suitable for the general defence of the community against invasion or oppression, and the secret carrying of those suited merely to deadly individual encounters may be prohibited." (Const. Law, 2d ed., pp. 282, 283). So, too, it has been declared that the arms to which the Second Amendment refers include weapons of warfare to be used in defending the State and civil liberty—but not pistols and such other weapons as are habitually carried by those who, in the vernacular of today, are termed gangsters. (State v. Workman, 35 W. Va. 367, 373; cf. People v. Persee, 204 N.Y. 397, 403.) To the same effect are decisions in other jurisdictions where citizens, invoking constitutional guaranties of the right to bear arms, have insisted that they were free to carry concealed weapons. (Nunn v. State, 1 Kelly [Ga.] 243; Aymette v. State, 2 Humph. [Tenn.] 154; State v. Buzzard, 4 Ark. 18; Andrews v. State, 3 Heisk. [Tenn.] 165; State v. Shelby, 90 Mo. 302; State v. Keet, 269 Mo. 206; Notes, L.R.A. 1917 C, p. 60.)[80]

Accordingly the New York court found:

> 2. The right of the people to bear arms, under section 4 of the Civil Rights Law, invoked by petitioner, is not infringed by laws prohibiting the carrying of concealed weapons. Furthermore, under similar statutes it is generally considered that the "arms" which are referred to include arms to be used in defending the State and civil liberty, but not pistols and weapons habitually carried by gangsters.
>
> 3. Petitioner acquired no vested right to a permit by virtue of the granting to him of earlier licenses to carry a pistol.[81]

The lone dissent set forth no decisional law, only the dissenter's evisceral reaction:

HILL, P. J. (dissenting). The order should be reversed and the prayer of the petition granted. The several statutes which are known collectively as the Sullivan Law, were enacted in an effort to prevent, or make more difficult, the obtaining of weapons by the criminal classes or by those who might use them in connection with crime. If the statute is extended beyond that scope and field, it is unconstitutional and infringes the right of the people to keep and bear arms. The need of the citizens to become proficient in the use of firearms is now brought strikingly to our attention. Six hundred thousand of our citizens in cities have sat in shelters at the top of tall buildings and in the country on lonely hillsides every hour, day and night, for more than eighteen months. Unless the home defense authorities were foolishly and unnecessarily panic-stricken there was some danger, no matter how slight, that a foreign foe would land or disloyal residents would take to the air in a hostile way. Under those circumstances, a man of the type of this petitioner who could shoot with accuracy, would be a more useful citizen than one who, if attacked, could only throw a bootjack at his assailant.

NOTES

1. The Purposes and Objectives of The National Rifle Association:

1. To protect and defend the Constitution of the United States, especially with reference to the inalienable right of the individual American citizen guaranteed by such Constitution to acquire, possess, transport, carry, transfer ownership of, and enjoy the right to use arms, in order that the people may always be in a position to exercise their legitimate individual rights of self-preservation and defense of family, person, and property, as well as to serve effectively in the appropriate militia for the common defense of the Republic and the individual liberty of its citizens;

2. To promote public safety, law and order, and the national defense;

3. To train members of law enforcement agencies, the armed forces, the militia, and the people of good repute in marksmanship and in the safe handling and efficient use of small arms;

4. To foster and promote the shooting sports, including the advancement of amateur competitions in marksmanship at the local, state, regional, national, and international levels;

5. To promote hunter safety, and to promote and defend hunting as a shooting sport and as a viable and necessary method of fostering the propagation, growth, conservation, and wise use of our renewable wildlife resources.

The Association may take all actions necessary and proper in the furtherance of these purposes and objectives. (This statement of NRA purposes and objectives is taken directly from Article II, NRA Bylaws.)

The following articles support the position of the National Rifle Association and "the right to keep and bear arms":

Blackman, Paul H., "Civil Liberties and Gun-Law Enforcement: Some Implications of Expanding the Powers of Police to Enforce a 'Liberal' Victimless Crime," paper presented at the annual meeting of the American Society of Criminology, Cincinnati, Ohio, November 7-11, 1984.

———, "Carrying Handguns for Personal Protection: Issues of Research and Public Policy," paper presented at the annual meeting of the American Society of Criminology, San Diego, Calif., November 13-16, 1985.

Bordua, David J., "Adversary Polling and the Construction of Social Meaning: Implications in Gun Control Elections in Massachusetts and California," *Law & Policy Quarterly* 5 (July 1983): 345-366.

Bruce-Biggs, Barry, "The Great American Gun War," *Public Interest,* No. 45 (Fall 1976): 37-62.

Cantrell, Charles L., "The Right to Bear Arms: A Reply," *Wisconsin Bar Bulletin* 53 (October 1980): 21-26.

Caplan, David I., "Restoring the Balance: The Second Amendment Revisited," *Fordham Urban Law Journal* 5 (Fall 1976): 31-53.

———, "Handgun Control: Constitutional or Unconstitutional?" *North Carolina Central Law Journal* 5 (Fall 1976): 53-58.

———, "The Right of the Individual to Bear Arms: A Recent Judicial Trend," *Detroit College of Law Review* (Winter 1982): 789-823.

Dowlut, Robert, "The Right to Arms: Does the Constitution or the Predilection of Judges Reign?" *Oklahoma Law Review* 36 (1983): 65-105.

———, "The Current Relevancy of Keeping and Bearing Arms," *University of Baltimore Law Forum* 15 (Fall 1984): 29-32.

———, and Janet Knoop, "State Constitutions and the Right to Keep and Bear Arms," *Oklahoma City University Law Review* 36 (1983): 177-241.

Gardiner, Richard E., "To Preserve Liberty—A Look at the Right to Keep and Bear Arms," *Northern Kentucky Law Review* 4 (1981): 63-96.

Halbrook, Stephen P., "The Jurisprudence of the Second and Fourteenth Amendments," *George Mason University Law Review* 4 (1981): 1-69.

———, "To Keep and Bear Their Private Arms: The Adoption of the Second Amendment 1789-1791," *Northern Kentucky Law Review* 10 (1982): 13-39.

———, "Tort Liability for the Manufacture, Sale, and Ownership of Handguns?" *Hamline Law Review* 6 (1983): 351-382.

———, *That Every Man Be Armed—The Evolution of a Constitutional Right.* Albuquerque: University of New Mexico Press, 1984.

———, "The Right to Bear Arms in the First State Bills of Rights: Pennsylvania, North Carolina, Vermont and Massachusetts," *Vermont Law Review* 10 (1985): 255-320.

Hardy, David T., "Firearms Ownership and Regulation; Tackling an Old Problem with Renewed Vigor," *William and Mary Law Review* 20 (1978): 255-290.

———, "Legal Restrictions of Firearms Ownership as an Answer to Violent Crime: What Was the Question?" *Hamline Law Review* 6 (1983): 391-408.

———, "Armed Citizens, Citizen Armies: Toward a Jurisprudence of the Second Amendment," *Harvard Journal of Law and Public Policy* (1986): 599-638.

———, *Origin and Development of the Second Amendment,* Southport, Conn.: Blacksmith Corporation, 1986.

———, and John Stompoly, "Of Arms and the Law," *Chicago-Kent Law Review* 51 (1974): 62-114.

Kates, Don B., Jr., ed., "Firearms and Firearms Regulation; Old Premises, New Research" (a symposium), *Law & Policy Quarterly* 5 (July 1983).

———, ed., *Restricting Handguns: The Liberal Skeptics Speak Out*, Croton-on-Hudson, N.Y.: North River Press, 1979.

———, ed., *Firearms and Violence: Issues of Public Policy*, Pacific Studies in Public Policy. Cambridge, Mass.: Ballinger, 1984.

———, special ed., "Gun Control" (a symposium), *Law and Contemporary Problems* 49 (Winter 1986): 1-267.

Kleck, Gary, and David Bordua, "The Factual Foundation for Certain Key Assumptions of Gun Control," *Law & Policy Quarterly* 5 (1983): 271-293.

———, "Policy Lessons from Recent Gun Control Research," *Law & Contemporary Problems* 49 (Winter 1986): 35-62.

Kukla, Robert, *Gun Control*. Harrisburg, Pa.: Stackpole Books, 1973.

Lizotte, Alan J., David J. Bordua, and Carolyn S. White, "Firearms Ownership for Sport and Protection: Two Not so Divergent Models," *American Sociological Review* 46 (August 1981): 499-503.

Malcolm, Joyce Lee, "The Right of the People to Keep and Bear Arms: The Common Law Tradition," *Hastings Constitutional Law Quarterly* 10 (1983): 285-314.

———, *Disarmed: The Loss of the Right to Bear Arms in Restoration England*. Cambridge, Mass.: The Mary Ingraham Bunting Institute of Radcliffe College, 1980.

Murray, Douglas P., "Handguns, Gun Control Laws and Firearms Violence," *Social Problems* 23 (1975): 81-93.

Santarelli, Donald F., and Nicholas Calio, "Turning the Gun on Tort Law," *St. Mary's Law Review* 14 (1983): 471-508.

Shalhope, Robert E., "The Idealogical Origins of the Second Amendment," *The Journal of American History* 69 (December 1982): 559-614.

Tonso, William R., *Guns and Society: The Social and Existential Roots of the American Attachment to Firearms*. Washington, D.C.: University Press of America, 1982.

U.S. Congress, Senate. Committee on the Judiciary, Subcommittee on the Constitution, *The Right to Keep and Bear Arms*, 97th Cong., 2d sess., 1982.

Weiss, Jonathan A., "A Reply to Advocates of Gun Control Law," *Journal of Urban Law* 52 (Winter 1974): 577-589.

Whisker, James B., *The Citizen Soldier and United States Military Policy*. Croton-on-Hudson, N.Y.: North River Press, 1979.

———, *Our Vanishing Freedom: The Right to Keep and Bear Arms*. McLean, Va.: Heritage House, 1972.

———, "Historical Development and Subsequent Erosion of the Right to Keep and Bear Arms," *West Virginia Law Review* 78 (1976): 171-190.

Wright, James, et al., *Under the Gun: Weapons, Crime and Violence in America*. New York: Aldine Publishing Co., 1983.

———, and Peter H. Rossi, *Armed and Considered Dangerous: A Survey of Felons and Their Firearms*. New York: Aldine DeGruyter, 1986.

2. Annals of Congress 434 (1789). See also Report of the Subcommittee on the Constitution of the Committee on the Judiciary, U.S. Senate, 97th

Congress, 2nd Sess., February 1982, entitled "The Right to Keep and Bear Arms," at p. 6.

3. 92 US 542 (1876).

4. See Steinberg, "Does the Second Amendment Mean What It Says?" Engage/Social Action (May 1977).

5. Infra note 2 Report at p. 83.

6. Roscoe Pound, The Development of Constitutional Guarantees of Liberty 91 (1957).

7. See 9 Hamline L Rev 69 (1986) at pp. 69-70.

8. See 82 Mich L Rev 204 (Nov. 1983) at p. 214.

9. See Maitland, The Constitutional History of England 276 (ed. 1961).

10. "An Act for the Better Security of the Inhabitants by Obliging the Male White Persons to Carry Fire Arms to Places of Public Worship, 1770," reprinted in 1775-1780 Georgia Colonial Laws 471 (1932).

11. 1 Stat 271 (1792). The argument is made that since Article I, Section 10, clause 3, of the Constitution forbids the states to raise "troops" or formal military units, this 1792 congressional statute would be unconstitutional if "militia" meant a formal military unit and not simply a body of citizen soldiers.

12. 564 F2d 387 (10th Cir., 1977).

13. Vietnamese Fishermen's Association v. Knights, 345 F Supp 198 (SD Tex., 1982).

14. See Presser v. Illinois, 116 US 252 (1886) at p. 265.

15. See Hast Const L Q 961 (1975).

16. Under 29 Op Att'y Gen 332 (1912) the militia may not be called for foreign duty; but as delineated in 54 Harv L Rev 181 (1940) at pp. 204-205 militia have been called for military service abroad. Note the words of Congressman Elbridge Gerry of Massachusetts speaking in 1789:

> What, sir, is the use of a militia? It is to prevent the establishment of a standing army, the bane of liberty. Now, it must be evident that, under this provision, together with their other powers, Congress could take such measures with respect to a militia, as to make a standing army necessary. Whenever Governments mean to invade the rights and liberties of the people, they always attempt to destroy the militia, in order to raise an army upon their ruins. This was done actually by Great Britain at the commencement of the late Revolution. They used every means in their power to prevent the establishment of an effective militia to the Eastward. The Assembly of Massachusetts, seeing the rapid progress that administration were making to devest them of their inherent privileges, endeavored to counteract them by the organization of a militia; but they were always defeated by the influence of the Crown. (1 Annals of Congress 749-750, August 17, 1789)

17. 72 Kan 230, 83 P 619 (1905).

18. 520 A2d 1057 (D.C. Cir., 1986).

19.

In previous decisions upholding firearms statutes in the District of Columbia against constitutional challenges, we have not addressed second amendment concerns. Williams v. United States, 237 A.2d 539 (D.C., 1968) (court will not consider second amendment challenge raised for the first time on appeal); Scott v. United States, 243 A.2d 54 (D.C., 1968) (holding that statute is not void for vagueness); McIntosh v. Washington, 395 A.2d 744, 754-57 (D.C., 1978) (ruling against appellant who raised defenses based on due process, equal protection, vagueness, and the burdening of interstate commerce); Fresjian v. Jefferson, 399 A.2d 861 (D.C., 1979) (denying equal protection and takings challenges). We now hold that D.C. Code arts. 6-2311, 6-2361, and 22-3204 (1981) do not violate the second amendment. We affirm appellant's convictions.

20. Infra note 18. Note the concurring opinion:

On the assumption which we make that the second amendment applies at all to District of Columbia, I concur in the opinion of the court. I write separately to state my conclusion that the second amendment does not apply to the seat of national government. This amendment is to ensure "the security of a free State." State militias were essential to that end—hence, the amendment. Nothing suggests that the founders were concerned about "free territories," "free protectorates" or a "free Seat of Government of the United States." See U.S. Const. art. I, Art 8, cl. 17. Indeed clause 17 gives to Congress exclusive legislative power in all cases over such "District." It may fairly be said that a federal militia is available in such places. Therefore, whatever may be said for the second amendment and its reach within the several states, I conclude first that it does not apply to the Seat of Government of the United States.

21. 1 Annals of Congress 434 (1789).

22. See Goebel, History of the Supreme Court of the United States 450 (1971); see also 10 No Ky L Rev 63 (1982) at p. 79.

23. 1 Ga 241 (1846) at p. 251.

24. See generally 38 U Chi L Rev 185 (1970).

25. Infra note 7 at p. 102.

26. See 1969 Duke L J 773 (1969) at pp. 796-797.

27. Cf. Cooley, General Principles of Constitutional Law in the United States of America (3rd ed., 1898) at pp. 298-299:

It may be supposed from the phraseology of this provision that the right to keep and bear arms was only guaranteed to the militia; but this would be an interpretation now warranted by the intent. The militia, as has been elsewhere explained, consists of those persons who, under the law, are liable to the performance of military duty, and are officered and enrolled for service when called upon. But the law may make provision for the enrollment of all or who are fit to perform military duty, or of a small number only, or it may wholly omit to make any provision at all; and if the right were limited to those enrolled, the purpose of this guaranty might be defeated altogether by the action or neglect to act of the government it was meant to hold in check. The meaning of the provision undoubtedly is, that the people, from whom the militia must be taken, shall have the right to keep and bear arms, and they need no permission or regulation of law for the purpose. But this enables the government to have a well regulated militia; for to bear arms implies something more than the mere keeping; it implies the learning to handle and use them in a way that makes those who keep them ready for their efficient use; in other words, it implies the right to meet for voluntary discipline in arms, observing in doing so the laws of public order.

28. See Okla L Rev 65 (1983) at p. 96.
29. See 82 Mich L Rev 204 (1983) at p. 267.
30. 307 US 174 (1939).
31. 131 F2d 916 (lst Cir., 1942), cert den 319 US 770 (1942).
32. 407 US 143 (1972).
33. Note Lewis v. United States, 445 US 95 (1980), in which the Court cited favorably that same view as it upheld the 1968 Gun Control Act.
34. 82 Mich L Rev 204 (1983) at p. 259.
35. 695 F2d 261 (7th Cir., 1982), cert den 104 S Ct 194 (1983).
36. State v. Kessler, 289 Ore 359, 614 P2nd 94 (1980).
37. See 2 Bishop, Commentaries on the Criminal Law Section 124 (Boston, 1865).
38. Infra note 28 at p. 99.
39. Whether the Second Amendment is applicable to the states through the Fourteenth Amendment is open to question; see 4 Geo Mason L Rev 1 (1981).
40. Note that these thirteen states are scattered throughout the country and embrace every section of the nation including the most populated areas as well as sparsely populated areas. See generally 4 Detroit C Law Rev 789 (1982).
41. Ala. Const., Art. I, Section 26.
42. Ariz. Const., Art. II, Section 26.
43. Colo. Const., Art. II, Section 13.
44. Conn. Const., Art. I, Section 15.
45. Ill. Const., Art. I, Section 22.
46. La. Const., Art. I, Section 4.
47. Me. Const., Art. 1, Section 16.
48. Mich. Const., Art. I, Section 6.
49. Miss. Const., Art. III, Section 12.
50. Mo. Const., Art. I, Section 23.
51. Mont. Const., Art. II, Section 12.
52. N.M. Const., Art. II, Section 6.
53. Okla. Const., Art. II, Section 26.
54. Texas Const., Art. I, Section 23.
55. Wash. Const., Art. I, Section 24.
56. Alas. Const., Art. I, Section 19.
57. Ark. Const., Art. II, Section 5.
58. Fla. Const., Art. I, Section 8.
59. Ga. Const., Art. I, Section 1.
60. Haw. Const., Art. 1, Section 15.

66. Idaho Const., Art. 1, Section 11.
62. Ind. Const., Art. 1, Section 32.
63. Kans. Const., Bill of Rights, Section 4.
64. Ky. Const., Section 1.
65. Mass. Const., pt. 1, Art. 17.
66. N.C. Const., Art. 1, Section 30.
67. Ohio Const., Art. 1, Section 4.
68. Ore. Const., Art. 1, Section 27.
69. Pa. Const., Art. 1, Section 21.
70. R.I. Const., Art. 1, Section 22.
71. S.C. Const., Art. 1, Section 20.
72. S.D. Const., Art. 6, Section 24.
73. Tenn. Const., Art. 1, Section 26.
74. Utah Const., Art 1, Section 6.
75. Vt. Const., ch. 1, Art. 16.
76. Va. Const., Art. 1, Section 13.
77. Wyo. Const., Art. 1, Section 24.
78. 450 So2d 1212 (Fla. App., 1984).
79. The court explained its decision:

Section 790.01(2) makes it a third degree felony to carry a concealed firearm on or about one's person. Prior to amendment in 1982, section 790.25 (3)(1) made an exception merely for "[a]ny person traveling by private conveyance when the weapon is securely encased." In Ensor v. State, 403 So.2d 349 (Fla. 1981), the Supreme Court of Florida held that a firearm need not be absolutely invisible in order to be concealed, for purposes of the statute prohibiting carrying a concealed firearm, so long as the weapon was concealed from the casual and ordinary observation of another in the normal associations of life, and the weapon was physically on the person or readily accessible to its bearer. Thus a passenger in a vehicle was carrying a concealed weapon when an officer who stopped the vehicle, peering through the windshield, saw a portion of a white object which he was then able to tell, by looking into the already-opened passenger door, was a derringer. According to Ensor a firearm could simultaneously be in open view, for purposes of seizure under the open view doctrine, and concealed, in violation of the concealed firearms statute. Moreover, even if a weapon were in a locked glove compartment, Ensor indicated it could be "about the person" and thus a prohibited concealed weapon.

Ensor apparently prompted the legislature to add section 790.25(5), Florida Statutes (Supp. 1982), which provides:

(5) POSSESSION IN PRIVATE CONVEYANCE.—Notwithstanding subsection (2), it is lawful and is not a violation of s. 790.01 to possess a concealed firearm or other weapon for self-defense or other lawful purpose within the interior of a private conveyance, without a license, if the firearm or other weapon is securely encased or is otherwise not readily accessible for immediate use. Nothing herein contained prohibits the carrying of a legal firearm other than a handgun anywhere in a private conveyance when such firearm is being carried for a lawful use. Nothing herein contained shall be construed to authorize

the carrying of a concealed firearm or other weapon on the person. This subsection shall be liberally construed in favor of the lawful use, ownership, and possession of firearms and other weapons, including lawful self-defense as provided in s. 776.012. Subsection (2), mentioned in the quoted subsection, makes clear that the usual requirement of a permit to carry a concealed firearm is not undone by this portion of the statute. The 1982 legislature also provided definitions for ''securely encased'' and ''readily accessible for immediate use.'' '' 'Securely encased' means encased in a glove compartment, whether or not locked; in a snapped holster; in a gun case, whether or not locked; in a zippered gun case; or in a closed box or container which requires a lid or cover to be opened for access.'' Section 790.001 (16), Florida Statutes (Supp. 1982). '' 'Readily accessible for immediate use' means that a firearm or other weapon is carried on the person or within such close proximity and in such a manner that it can be retrieved and used as easily and quickly as if carried on the person.'' Section 790.000 (15), Florida Statutes (Supp. 1982).

80. 45 NYS2d 63 (1943).

81. ''Petitioner's assertion of a vested right acquired by him through the granting of earlier licenses is untenable in the light of this utterance by the Court of Appeals: ''A power to grant a privilege to one is inconsistent with the possession on the part of another of an absolute right to exercise such privilege. The requirement that a person must secure leave from some one to entitle him to exercise a right, carries with it, by natural implication, a discretion on the part of the other to refuse to grant it, if, in his judgment, it is improper or unwise to give the required consent.'' (People ex rel. Schwab v. Grant, 126 NY 473, 481.)

3

Historical Perspective on Keeping and Bearing Arms

3.1 ARMS AND THE MAN BEFORE 1787

While the National Rifle Association of America and advocates of the individual right to keep and bear arms prefer to base their historical argument on what transpired from the Stone Age to the present day, it is more sensible to confine the historical perspective to England and colonial America. The first limitation in England on the right of a law-abiding person to keep and bear arms was probably the 1181 Statute of Assize of Arms, which prohibited the possession of and ordered the disposition of all coats of mail or breastplates in the hands of Jews in England.[1] This religiously discriminating statute was followed some 200 years later by the 1328 Statute of Northampton, which banned all private persons from using any force in public "in affray of the peace" or from going or riding armed in public.[2] But English courts were reluctant to enforce such intrusions upon the principle of allowing "gentlemen to ride armed for their security,"[3] and required proof of criminal or evil intent. Subsequent eighteenth-century English decisions recognized the right to keep guns in the home for self-defense as well as the right to carry ordinary arms in public in a peaceful manner. But the Militia Act of 1662 empowered the king to authorize searches of the person and the home and to "seize all arms in the custody or possession" of dangerous persons.[4] The 1689 English Bill of Rights[5] provided that it was necessary for public safety that "the Subjects which are Protestants may have Arms for their Defence, suitable to their Condition, and as allowed by Law.''[6] This right of self-defense was apparently found in the law of nature and ''is not, nor can be, superseded by any law of society.''[7] It is remarkable that this right to keep and bear arms had not been included in the Magna Carta, the Petition of Right, or any compilation of the rights of Englishmen before 1689.[8] One possible explanation may lie in a recognition that perhaps there is another view of the origin of the right to keep and bear arms, that is, a hybrid position[9] that recognizes both the individual right[10] and the collective right.[11] It is pointed out that the framers of the U.S. Constitution did not propose to protect the militia nor to safeguard individual arms. In short, the ''hybrid'' position holds that neither the collective nor the individual school of thought is correct insofar as these views attempt to explain entirely the Second Amendment.[12] According to the note writer,[13] ''the Second Amendment's militia component and its right to bear arms recognition have in fact different origins and theoretical underpinnings. One is a legacy of the Renaissance . . . and the other is the creation of 17th century English experience. . . . At the time of the framing of our Constitution, the militia statement found its primary constituency among the gentry, particularly that of Virginia. The individual right to bear arms provision was primarily advanced by the Radical movement, particularly in Pennsylvania and Massachusetts. Only after the Constitution had received its crucial ninth ratification were the two precepts joined into a single sentence, thereby creating a constitutional 'package' which addressed the demands of both schools of thought. . . . The Second Amendment therefore has historical interest which extends beyond militia and arms issues. It is, metaphorically speaking, a fault line in the bedrock of the Constitution; the one place where a rough joinder of related ideas enables us today to discern a turning point between two entirely different American approaches to statecraft.''[14]

3.2 ARMS AND THE MAN AFTER 1787

In colonial America there was always the presence of the Indian, who was not only the victim of invasions by the colonists, the French, the Dutch, and the Spanish, but was a threat to the security of the colonists. Colonists were soldiers because they lived on the battlefield, and their reliance on arms was a truism that governed their very lives. The colonial militia system subjected virtually all males to militia service and required that the militiamen furnish themselves with arms and ammunition.[15] Colonial law also required persons exempt from militia training to keep arms and ammunition at home. After the American Revolutionary War the winning ex-colonists commenced to write a constitution that would be a product of their experiences. One of the many problems confronting the delegates to the convention in Philadelphia was how to reconcile the fear of a standing army, which was inimical to personal freedom and liberty, with the need to defend the fledgling nation. Under Article I, Section 8, of the Constitution the military was precluded from accruing too much power by recognition that the Congress had the authority to raise a standing army; the militia could be called forth "to execute the laws of the Union, suppress Insurrections, and repel Invasions." Although a state could not "keep troops" without congressional consent,[16] the delegates did limit the authority of Congress over state militia to those times when the militia were employed in federal service.[17] On the right to bear arms the earliest proposal by Pennsylvania that "the people have a right to bear arms for the defense of themselves and their own state, or the United States or for the purpose of killing game" was soundly defeated along with other proposals for a bill of rights.[18] Indeed, the proposed bill of rights requiring a two-thirds majority of each house of Congress and three-quarters of the states was not easy to come by, although the proposal on the right to keep and bear arms was considered to be one of the least controversial. Owning, collecting, and using guns in the early days after 1787 was universal; President George Washington is estimated to have owned more than fifty firearms including rifles, shotguns, and pistols, and even James Madison, the chief writer of the Bill of Rights, collected firearms.[19] Ownership of firearms was deemed a basis of character and citizenship. The initial draft in June 1789 of the Second Amendment by James Madison stated, "A well regulated militia, composed of the body of the people, being the best security of a free state, the right of the people to keep and bear arms shall not be infringed; but no person religiously scrupled shall be compelled to bear arms."[20] The latter part on conscientious objection to military service was deleted in the Senate, and the final product was shortened by deletion of the phrase "composed of the body of people" and the phrase on security was modified to read "necessary to the security of a free state." After Congress adopted the amendments, the ratification struggle in the states lasted for the next two years, although the right to keep and bear arms was not an issue. As reflected in the *Gazette of the United States,* "the right of the people to keep and bear arms has been recognized by the General Government; but the best security of that right after all is the military spirit, that taste for martial exercises, which has always distinguished the free citizens of these States"[21] President George Washington in 1790 reminded members of the House of Representatives that "a free people ought not only to be armed, but disciplined."[22] An 1825 publication, "View of the Constitution," observed with respect to the Second Amendment that "no clause in the Constitution could by a rule of construction be conceived to give to Congress a power to disarm the people. Such a flagitious attempt could only be made under some general pretense by a state legislature. But if in blind pursuit of inordinate power, either should attempt it, this amendment may be appealed to as a restraint on both."[23]

It is of more than passing interest that there might never have been a federal Bill of Rights had it not been for Article V of the Constitution which sanctioned a second federal convention called by the states to revise the document.[24] New York Governor DeWitt Clinton wrote the circular letter making this proposal to the governors of all the states. Ratification of the Bill of Rights was finally achieved on December 15, 1791.

3.3 STATES AND EARLY CONSTITUTIONS AND BILLS OF RIGHTS

The state constitutions framed during the American Revolutionary War reflected, at least with respect to the Second Amendment, the real fears of the legislators concerning a standing army that would impinge upon their newly won freedoms.[25]The replacement of the standing army with a popular state militia was believed to remove arbitrary military power from the hands of the federal government and to place that power in the hands of civil authorities and the people at large. Indeed, it was understood that having a right to bear arms would enable the people to possess far greater military power than if the militia were merely the preferred modus operandi. In short, the right to bear arms was an affirmation that the people collectively had control over the situation about a standing army and militia.[26]

Admittedly, "a constitution is not to receive a technical or strained construction, but rather the words should be interpreted in their popular, natural and ordinary meaning. We should also consider the circumstances attending its formation and the construction probably placed upon it by the people.''[27] The Pennsylvania court in Commonwealth v. Ray emphasized that the right to bear arms is ''a constitutional one and cannot be diminished by any act of the Legislature.''[28] But it is not clear whether the language of a state constitution is so impervious to change or interpretation that its words are chiseled in stone. The same Philadelphia ordinance regulating the purchase of firearms was successfully upheld in the federal court on Second Amendment grounds. The Third U.S. Court of Appeals rejected the appellant's argument that under the Second Amendment he is entitled to bear arms and ruled that ''appellant is completely wrong about that. . . . It must be remembered that the right to keep and bear arms is not a right given by the United States Constitution.''[29] An early Georgia decision, Hill v. State,[30] upholding a conviction for being armed in court, viewed the early Georgia constitution in these words:

> The right to bear or carry arms about the person at all times and places and under all circumstances is not a necessity for the declared object of the guarantee; nay, that it does not even tend to secure the great purpose sought for, to wit: that the people shall be familiar with the use of arms and capable from their habits of life, of becoming efficient militiamen. . . . The right to keep and to bear arms so that the state may be secured in the existence a well regulated militia is fully attained. The people have or may have the arms the public exigencies require, and being unrestricted in the bearing and using them, except under special and peculiar circumstances, there is no infringement of the constitutional guarantee.[31]

It is interesting to note that the constitutions of New Jersey of 1776 and of Georgia the following year contained no bill of rights that could have delineated the right to keep and bear arms.[32] Court decisions in Pennsylvania and Vermont, for example, have construed the right to bear arms ''for the defense of themselves and the State.''[33] Massachusetts courts have narrowly interpreted the constitutional provision that ''the people have a right to keep and bear arms for the common defense.''[34] On the other hand, an 1843 ruling in a court in North Carolina (whose original Declaration of Rights was similar to the Massachusetts constitutional provision) gave the right to keep and bear arms an individual dimension: ''The bill of rights in this State secures to every man . . . a right of which he cannot be deprived. . . . The carrying of a gun, per se, constitutes no offense.''[35] In 1921 in State v. Kerner the North Carolina Supreme Court blood-thirstily described ''a sacred right based upon the experience of the ages in order that the people may be accustomed to bear arms and ready to use them for the protection of their liberties or their country when occasion serves. . . . Had not the common people, the rank and file, those who 'bore the burden of battle' during our great Revolution, been accustomed to the use of arms, the victories for liberty would not have been won and American independence would have been an impossibility.''[36] Yet forty-seven years later the same court in State v. Dawson interpreted the North Carolina arms guarantee as *both* a collective and an individual right: ''While the purpose of the constitutional guaranty of the right to bear arms was to secure a well regulated militia and not an individual's right to have a weapon in order to exercise his common law right of self-defense, . . . North Carolina decisions have interpreted our Constitution as guaranteeing the right to bear arms to the people in a collective sense, similar to the concept of a militia . . . and also to individuals.''[37]

The constitutions of Maryland and Delaware did not include arms guarantees[38] and South Carolina's Constitution of 1776 similarly had no bill of rights or concern about arms guarantees.[39] New York even today has no constitutional provision on the right to keep and bear arms.[40] Only the Virginia Declaration of Rights of 1776 heralded the virtues of ''a well regulated Militia, composed of the body of People, trained to Arms.''[41]

3.4 MODERN SCIENCE OF WEAPONS TECHNOLOGY

It is perfectly obvious that the founders of this country, the framers of the Constitution and the drafters of the Second Amendment, could not have anticipated modern weaponry, nuclear arms, and anti-aircraft missiles. The Second Amendment, whether judged as an individual or as a collective right, simply must be reviewed critically as to whether the so-called right to keep and bear arms realistically applies to modern weaponry. In view of worldwide terrorist activities, the carrying of a private weapon, whether simple or complex, ancient or modern, in areas of special sensitivity such as airports, subways, courthouses, and public buildings, must be prohibited. These restrictions in the modern day make somewhat futile the exercise of the so-called right to keep and bear arms. It is more than regulation to ban arms in these sensitive areas; it is almost a repudiation that the Second Amendment has any relevancy today to any individual's right to keep and bear arms. Only the collective right interpretation makes any sense in the modern era, and legislatures should readily ban the possession of dangerous weapons by private citizens where circumstances warrant such action. States are not restricted by the Second Amendment and can take the requisite action.[42] The contrary view is seen in State v. Kessler, where the Oregon court indicated that it was "not unmindful that there is current controversy over the wisdom of a right to bear arms, and that the original motivations for such a provision might not seem compelling if debated as a new issue";[43] but the court nevertheless struck down the law as impinging upon the antiquated Second Amendment. The "ideological heirs of the vigilantes of the bygone western frontier era"[44] continue to oppose state legislative control of handguns and rifles, despite the clearcut fact that the Second Amendment was designed solely to protect the states against the general government, not to create a personal right that either the state or the federal authorities are bound to respect.

NOTES

1. See Stubbs, Select Charters and Other Illustrations of English Constitutional History 154 (8th ed., 1900).
2. 2 Edw 3, ch 3 (1328); see 4 Detroit C L Rev 789 (1982).
3. See Rex v. Knight, 90 Eng Re 330 (K.B., 1696) at p. 330.
4. 13 & 14 Car 2, ch 3 (1662).
5. 1 W & M Sess 2, ch 2 (1689).
6. 14 H L Jour 125 (1689).
7. See Foster, Crown Cases 273-274 (London, 1776); also 7 Okla City U L Rev (1982) at p. 183.
8. See Malcolm, Disarmed: The Loss of the Right to Bear Arms in Restoration England (1980) at p. 24.
9. See generally Hardy, "The Second Amendment and the Historiography of the Bill of Rights," 4 J of Law & Pol 1 (Summer 1987).
10. Caplan, "The Right of the Individual to Bear Arms: A Recent Judicial Trend," 1982 Det CL Rev 789; Dowlut, "The Right to Arms: Does the Constitution or the Predilection of Judges Reign?" 36 Okla. L Rev 65 (1983); Dowlut & Knoop, "State Constitutions and the Right to Keep and Bear Arms," 7 Okla City U L Rev 177 (1982); S. Halbrook, That Every Man Be Armed: The Evolution of a Constitutional Right (1984); Subcomm. on the Constitution

of the Sen. Judiciary Comm., The Right to Keep and Bear Arms, 97th Cong., 2d Sess. (Comm. Print 1982); Halbrook, "The Right to Bear Arms in the First State Bills of Rights: Pennsylvania, North Carolina, Vermont, and Massachusetts," 10 Vt L Rev 255 (1985) [hereinafter The Right to Bear Arms]; Halbrook, "To Keep and Bear Their Private Arms: The Adoption of the Second Amendment 1787-1791," 10 N Ky L Rev 13 (1982); Hardy, "Armed Citizens, Citizen Armies: Toward a Jurisprudence of the Second Amendment," 9 Harv J of Law & Pub Pol 559 (1986) [hereinafter Armed Citizens]; D. Hardy, Origins and Development of the Second Amendment (1986); Kates, "Handgun Prohibition and the Original Meaning of the Second Amendment," 82 Mich L Rev 204 (1983); Malcolm, "The Right of the People to Keep and Bear Arms: The Common Law Tradition," 10 Hastings Const L Q 285 (1983); and Shalhope, "The Ideological Origins of the Second Amendment," 69 J Am Hist 599 (1982).

11. Beschle, "Reconsidering the Second Amendment: Constitutional Protection for Right of Security," 9 Hamline L Rev 69 (1986); Cress, "An Armed Community: The Origins and Meaning of the Right to Bear Arms," 71 J Am Hist 22 (1984); Levin, "The Right to Bear Arms: The Development of the American Experience," 48 Chi-Kent L Rev 148 (1971); Note, "The Right to Bear Arms," 19 S C L Rev 402 (1967).

12. Infra note 9 at pp. 2-3.

13. Id.

14. Infra note 9 at p. 59:

> The Second Amendment to the Constitution had two objectives. The first purpose was to recognize in general terms the importance of a militia to a free state. This recognition derives from the very core of Classical Republican thought; its "constituency" among the Framers was found primarily among conservatives, particularly Virginia's landed gentry. Indeed, prior to Virginia's proposal, no federal ratifying convention had called for such recognition. The second purpose was to guarantee an individual right to own and carry arms. This right stemmed both from the English Declaration of Rights and from Enlightenment sources. Its primary supporters came from the Radical-Democratic movement, whether based among the small farmers of western Pennsylvania or the urban mechanics of Massachusetts. Only by incorporating both provisions could the first Congress reconcile the priorities of Sam Adams with those of George Mason, and lessen the "disquietude" both of the Pennsylvania and Massachusetts minorities and those of the Virginia and New York majorities. The dual purpose of the second amendment was recognized by all early constitutional commentators; the assumption that the second amendment had but a single objective is in fact an innovation born of historical ignorance.

15. See 1 The Colonial Laws of New York from the Year 1664 to the Revolution 231 (1894); also 36 Okla L Rev 65 (1983).

16. Article I, Section 10, cl. 3.

17. Article I, Section 8, cl. 16.

18. McMaster & Stone, Pennsylvania and the Federal Constitution 1787-1788 (ed. 1888) at p. 422.

19. See The American Rifleman (July 1981) at pp. 22-24.
20. 1 Annals of Congress 749 (ed., 1789).
21. Gazette of the United States (Oct. 14, 1789) at p. 211, col. 2.
22. Boston Independent Chronicle (Jan. 14, 1790) at p. 3.
23. William Rawle, A View of the Constitution 125-126 (2nd ed., Phila., (1803).
24. 2 Hastings Const L Q (Winter 1975) at pp. 163 et seq.
25. See Section 7 of Chapter 2 for an analysis of the fifty state constitutions today.
26. See generally Chi-Kent L Rev (Fall-Winter 1971) for the article by Professor John Levin, "The Right to Bear Arms: The Development of the American Experience."
27. Commonwealth of Pennsylvania v. Harmon, 469 Pa 490, 366 A2d 895 (1976) at pp. 490 and 897.
28. 218 Pa Super 72, 272 A2d 275 (1970); see generally 10 Vt L Rev 255 (1985).
29. Eckert v. City of Philadelphia, 329 F Supp 845 (ED Pa., 1973), aff 477 F2d 610 (3rd Cir., 1973), cert den 414 US 839 (1973).
30. 53 Ga 473 (1874).
31. Id.:

> The right to bear arms in order that the state may, when its exigencies demand, have at call a body of men, having arms at their command, belonging to themselves and habituated to the use of them, is in no fair sense a guarantee that the owners of these arms may bear them at concerts, and prayer-meetings, and elections. At such places, the bearing of arms of any sort, is an eye-sore to good citizens, offensive to peaceable people, an indication of a want of proper respect for the majesty of the laws, and a marked breach of good manners. If borne at all under the law, they must be borne openly and plainly exposed to view, and under the circumstances we allude to, the very act is not only a provocation to a breach of the peace, but dangerous to human life.

32. See Erdman, The New Jersey Constitution of 1776 (Princeton, 1929) at pp. 32-36, and The Constitution of the State of Georgia (Savannah, 1777).
33. See 10 Vt L Rev 255 (1985) at p. 261.
34. Opinion of the Justices, 80 Mass. 614 (1859).
35. State v. Huntley, 25 N.C. 284 (1843).
36. 181 N.C. 574, 107 SE 222 (1921).
37. 272 N.C. 644, 159 SE 1 (1968).
38. Infra note 33 at p. 317.
39. Id.
40. Infra note 30 in Chapter 2.
41. Va. Dec. of Rights, Article XIII (1776).
42. Miller v. Texas, 153 US 535 (1894). In Ex Parte Ramirez, 226 P 914

(Cal., 1924) it was made clear that the California legislature was "entirely free to deal with the subject."

43. 289 Ore. 359, 614 P2d 94 (1980).

44. 2 Hastings Const L Q (Winter 1975) at p. 169.

4

The Courts and the Second Amendment

4.1 U.S. SUPREME COURT DESICIONS OF NOTE

A review of decisions of the U.S. Supreme Court for the past 130 years or so reveals a dearth of instances where the Second Amendment was an issue. The Dred Scott case in 1857 is an early example where the Second Amendment was only parenthetically involved.[1] Here Chief Justice Roger B. Taney, in arguing that the framers of the Constitution could not have intended free black Americans to be citizens, cited, among other things, the right "to keep and bear arms wherever they went." This declaration by the highest court was hardly a ringing endorsement of the Second Amendment, much less support for the individual right view. Not until 1876 did the Court in United States v. Cruickshank more directly face the issue of the Second Amendment, although in reality the issue was civil rights legislation and not the right to bear arms or the militia.[2] The defendants had been convicted of conspiracy to deprive black citizens of the rights and privileges secured to them by the Constitution and laws of the United States in violation of the criminal provisions of the Civil Rights Act of 1870. Among those rights violated was the right to keep and bear arms for a lawful purpose. Chief Justice Waite, speaking for the majority of the Court, affirmed the dismissal of defendants' conviction and held that the rights that the defendants had violated were not secured by the Constitution or by the laws of the United States. The only rights protected, according to the Court, were those necessary for participation in the national government:

> The right . . . of 'bearing arms for a lawful purpose' . . . is not a right granted by the Constitution. Neither is it in any manner dependent upon that instrument for its existence. The Second Amendment declares that it shall not be infringed; but this, as has been seen, means no more than that it shall not be infringed by Congress. This is one of the amendments that has no other effect than to restrict the powers of the national government, leaving the people to look for their protection against any violation by their fellow-citizens of the rights it recognizes, to what is called . . . the powers which relate to merely municipal legislation, or what was, perhaps, more properly called internal police, "not surrendered or restrained" by the Constitution of the United States.[3]

The central point of the court opinion was not an endorsement of the personal or individual right to bear arms but a recognition that Congress could not infringe thereupon. The states, however, could pass whatever legislation they desired without fear of federal sanctions. At most, the court deemed the right to keep and bear arms to be "an attribute of citizenship under a free government."[4] This 1876 decision established that under the Second Amendment the right to keep and bear arms was a collective right exercised through the maintenance of a militia.[5] It is also significant that in the appeal to the U.S. Supreme Court neither the federal government nor the defendants had sought to incorporate the Second Amendment into the Fourteenth Amendment and thereby seek to prohibit the states from infringing upon the right to keep and bear arms.[6] The private infringement here did not involve state action, and the remedy for the statutory violations was available in state courts. It is said that the Cruickshank case refusing to protect the black's rights came to symbolize and perhaps hasten the end of the Reconstruction period in U.S. history.[7]

Exactly ten years later in 1886 Presser v. Illinois ascended to the U.S. Supreme Court.[8] Presser had led a parade of 400 armed men through the streets of Chicago, and the state of Illinois charged him with unlawfully assembling a military company and parading under arms without a license. The highest court upheld his conviction on the ground that the states could regulate such parades of armed men on public streets. Furthermore, the conviction of the defendant did not "infringe the right of the people to keep and bear arms." The Second Amendment is "a limitation only upon the power of Congress and the National government, and not upon the States. It was so held by this court on the case of United States v. Cruickshank."[9] The court also stressed that the Second Amendment is concerned only with military matters:

> The plaintiff in error was not a member of the organized volunteer militia of the State of Illinois, nor did he belong to the troops of the United States or to any organization under the militia law of the United States. On the contrary, the fact that he did not belong to the organized militia or the troops of the United States was an ingredient in the offense for which he was convicted and sentenced. The question is, therefore, had he a right as a citizen of the United States, in disobedience of the State law, to associate with others as a military company and to drill and parade with arms in the towns and cities of the State? If the plaintiff in error has any such privilege he must be able to point to the provision of the Constitution or statutes of the United States by which it is conferred.[10]

The obvious implication here is that any right to keep and bear arms by virtue of the Second Amendment, even if asserted against the federal government, is contingent upon military service in accordance with statutory law, for "the right to voluntarily associate together as a military company or organization, or to drill or parade with arms, without, and independent of, an act of Congress or law of the State authorizing the same, is not an attribute of national citizenship. Military organization and military drill and parade under arms are subjects especially under the control of government of every country. They cannot be claimed as a right independent of law."[11] Thus, the Second Amendment protects members of a state militia and protects them only against being disarmed by the federal government. There is simply no individual right to keep and bear arms that can be claimed independent of state militia law.[12]

In 1894 the highest court entertained Miller v. Texas, where a convicted murderer asserted that the state of Texas had violated his Second Amendment right to keep and bear arms by "forbidding the carrying of weapons."[13] The court curtly dismissed the appeal, hinting that, even if the right was an individual right, it was protected only against the federal government and not against the state government. Professors Alviani and Drake, cited in the November 1983 edition of the *Michigan Law Review,*[14] are quoted as stating that this decision is evidence that "the Second Amendment does not guarantee a personal right to own firearms. . . . Personal self-protection was never an issue in the adoption of the Second Amendment." Interestingly, neither party in Miller v. Texas[15] "set up in the trial court" the issue of whether the Fourteenth

Amendment "limited the power of the States as to such rights."[16] Accordingly, the court concluded that the Second Amendment "operate[s] only upon the Federal power, and [has] no reference whatever to proceedings in state courts."[17]

Three years later in 1897 Robertson v. Baldwin[18] dealt with the question of whether compulsory service of deserting seamen constituted involuntary servitude and treated the bearing of arms as a fundamental, centuries-old right that could not be infringed "by laws prohibiting the carrying of concealed weapons."[19] This judicial recognition did not mean that the court viewed the right to keep and bear arms as belonging to individuals; the state legislation on concealed weapons referred to the general public, not to individuals.

The case of United States v. Miller,[20] decided in 1939, involved a challenge to the National Firearms Act of 1934, which required registration of and a $200 tax upon transfers of certain arms, chiefly machine guns, "sawed-off" shotguns, and rifles.[21] The federal district court had dismissed a prosecution against the defendant who allegedly transported a "sawed-off" shotgun on grounds that the federal statute usurped the police power of the state and also violated the Second Amendment. The U.S. Supreme Court on a direct appeal reversed the dismissal and observed that the Second Amendment was purposefully drawn "to assure the continuation and render possible the effectiveness" of the militia and therefore "must be interpreted and applied with that end in view."[22] Thus, the highest court endorsed the collective right approach, and the right to keep and bear arms was to be limited to the organized militia. The federal government can regulate the possession of all arms that do not have a direct relationship to maintaining a well-regulated militia, for the Second Amendment defines and protects a collective right that is vested only in members of the state militia. The decision is indeed not limited to the "sawed-off" shotgun, as opponents to arms control believe.[23] As the First U.S. Court of Appeals expressed it three years later in Cases v. United States,[24] "to hold that the Second Amendment limits the federal government to regulations concerning only weapons which can be classed as antiques or curiosities—almost any other might bear some reasonable relationship to the preservation or efficiency of a well regulated militia unit of the present day—is in effect to hold that the limitation of Second Amendment is absolute."[25] The court recognized that such an interpretation would preclude the federal government from prohibiting private ownership of heavy weapons "even though under the circumstances of such possession or use it would be inconceivable that a private person could have any legitimate reason for having such a weapon.''[26] But the federal appellate court in Cases v. United States rejected the idea that individuals were part of the militia/nonmilitia weapons dichotomy, for no dichotomy was intended: ''We do not feel that the Supreme Court in this case was attempting to formulate a general rule applicable to all cases. The rule which it laid down was adequate to dispose of the case before it and that we think was as far as the Supreme Court intended to go.''[27]

In 1972 Justice William O. Douglas in E. Adams v. Williams had occasion to make an appropriate comment about pistols:

> A powerful lobby dins into the ears of our citizenry that these gun purchases are constitutional rights protected by the Second Amendment. . . . [But] there is under our decisions no reason why stiff State laws governing the purchase and possession of pistols may not be enacted. There is no reason why pistols may not be barred from anyone with a police record. There is no reason why a State may not require a purchaser of a pistol to pass a psychiatric test. There is no reason why all pistols should not be barred to everyone except the police. . . . Critics say that proposals like this water down the Second Amendment. Our decisions belie that argument, for the Second Amendment, as noted, was designed to keep alive the militia.''[28]

In 1980 the highest court in Lewis v. United States[29] upheld the 1968 Gun Control Act: ''these legislative restrictions on the use of firearms are neither based upon constitutionally suspect criteria, nor do they trench upon any constitutionally protected liberties.''[30]

4.2 FEDERAL APPELLATE COURT DECISIONS OF NOTE

Of the recent federal appellate decisions on the Second Amendment none stand out as formidable and challenging as Quilici v. Village of Morton Grove.[31] Here handgun owners challenged the constitutionality of an ordinance prohibiting handgun ownership within the Illinois village. The federal district court rejected plaintiffs' claim,[32] and the Seventh U.S. Court of Appeals in 1982 affirmed with important comment upon the scope of the Second Amendment: ''[It is] clear that the right to bear arms is inextricably connected to the preservation of a militia,'' and ''we do not consider individually owned handguns to be military weapons.'' Therefore, any private possession of arms not necessary for such militia functions is unprotected by the Second Amendment. The court regarded the historical background of bearing arms at common law and also at the time of the drafting of the Constitution as irrelevant.[33] Even the dissent of Judge Coffey did not explicitly favor the individual right approach, although admitting that "the right to possess commonly owned arms for self-defense" is a "basic human freedom"; it was the drastic total ban on the possession of such weapons that incurred the displeasure of the dissent, which regarded the "interference" with that freedom as the violation of the Constitution. The dissent did not rely on the Second Amendment, but cited the Fourth and Fifth Amendments and the rights of privacy[34] emanating from those provisions.[35]

Gun control enthusiasts, on the other hand, have achieved victories in the following representative federal appellate cases during the past sixteen or more years, as illustrated by the following compilation: (1st Cir.) United States v. Wilbur[36]; (3rd Cir.) Eckert v. City of Philadelphia[37]; (4th Cir.) United States v. Johnson[38]; (5th Cir.) McKnight v. United States[39]; (6th Cir.) Stevens v. United States[40]; (7th Cir.) United States v. Lauchli[41]; (8th Cir.) United States v. Synes[42]; (9th Cir.) United States v. Wynde [43]; and (10th Cir.) United States v. Oakes.[44]

4.3 STATE COURT DECISIONS OF NOTE

The volume of state court decisions delineating the Second Amendment has over the past years comprised a far greater proportion of the volume of U.S. Supreme Court and federal appellate court decisions.[45] For the most part, state court decisions have been more favorable to gun enthusiasts and the National Rifle Association of America as illustrated by the 1875 Texas Supreme Court decision in State of Texas v. Duke.[46] Here "arms" under the Texas Constitution was defined as more comprehensive than merely "arms of the militiaman or soldier," and therefore the defendant could not constitutionally be convicted for carrying a six-shooter pistol.

There are other examples of "NRA-appreciated" state court decisions. City of Lakewood v. Pillow upheld constitutional protection for "gunsmiths, pawnbrokers and sporting goods stores," which under the ordinance at issue would be prohibited "from carrying on a substantial part of their business. Also, the ordinance appears to prohibit individuals from transporting guns to and from such places of business.''[47] In People v. Liss the Illinois court stated that the Second Amendment ''provides the right of the people to keep and bear arms shall not be infringed. This, of course does not prevent the enactment of a law against carrying concealed weapons, but it does indicate it should keep in mind, in the construction of a statute of such character, that it is aimed at persons of criminal instincts, and for prevention of crime, and not against use in the protection of person or property.''[48] State v. Kessler pointed out that the term ''arms'' as used by the drafters of the constitutions probably was intended to include those weapons used by settlers for both personal and military defense. It was not limited to firearms but included several hand-carried weapons commonly used for defense. The term ''arms'' would not have included cannon and other heavy ordnance not kept by militiamen or private citizens.[49] Schubert v. DeBard refused to permit the state issuer of pistol-carrying licenses to look behind the applicant's stated reason of self-defense because the Indiana Constitution provides that ''the people shall have the right to bear arms, for the defense of themselves and the State.''[50] Taylor v. McNeal held that the pistols are not contraband because under the Missouri Constitution ''every citizen has the right to keep and bear arms in defense of his home, person, and property.''[51]

On the other hand, gun control advocates have won some victories in state courts. Commonwealth v. Davis pointed out that the Second Amendment could not restrict the states if the states choose to limit individual possession of weapons, since the avowed purpose of the Second Amendment was to protect the states against federal encroachment.[52] Salina v. Blaksley held that a collective right was guaranteed under the Kansas constitution's bill of rights providing that ''the people have the right to bear arms for their defense and security.'' Quilici v. Village of Morton Grove upheld the village ordinance that totally banned the private possession of all handguns within the village.[54]

4.4 THE FOURTEENTH AMENDMENT AND THE SECOND AMENDMENT

The Fourteenth Amendment in its pertinent clauses declares, ''No state shall make or enforce any law which shall abridge the privileges or immunities of citizens of the United States, nor shall any state deprive any person of life, liberty, or property without due process of law, nor deny to any person within its jurisdiction the equal protection of the laws.'' The prime question is whether the Fourteenth Amendment embodied the right to keep and bear arms of the Second Amendment, so that the states are precluded from enacting gun control legislation. Despite wishful thinking by the National Rifle Association of America and its millions of members, the Second Amendment has not yet been held applicable to the states, either directly or through incorporation of the Fourteenth Amendment. In United States v. Cruickshank[55] the U.S. Supreme Court in 1875 held that the Second Amendment restricts only Congress and the federal government, and this position was affirmed years later by the same court in Presser v. Illinois.[56] Indeed, the nature of the Second Amendment does not provide a right that could be interpreted as being incorporated into the Fourteenth Amendment. It was designed solely to protect the states against the federal or national government, not to create a personal right that either the state or federal authorities are bound to respect.[57]

The wishful thinkers favoring no control over guns would like to believe that the Fourteenth Amendment was enacted to protect the Second Amendment from *both* state and federal infringement. In fact, these zealots go so far as to state that all amendments or the entire bill of rights are binding on the states.[58] An 1846 Georgia case, Nunn v. State,[59] was unearthed for its totally supportive statement that ''the language of the Second Amendment is broad enough to embrace both Federal and State governments—nor is there anything in its terms which restricts its meaning.''[60] The Georgia court here had declared invalid a statutory prohibition on breast pistols; but two years later, in Cooper v. Savannah, the same court poignantly observed that ''free persons of color have never been recognized as citizens of Georgia, and they are not entitled to bear arms.''[61] Of course, the Fourteenth Amendment was not adopted as part of the Constitution until July 28, 1868, about twenty years later. These same zealots, however, point to an 1874 decision by the Georgia Supreme Court, Hill v. State,[62] which is supposed to stand for the proposition that ''the federal Constitution prohibits States from infringing on the fundamental right to possess either pistols or long guns.''[63]

The U.S. Supreme Court in the 1914 case of Patsone v. Pennsylvania considered whether a Pennsylvania statute making it unlawful for any unnaturalized foreign-born resident to own or possess a shotgun or rifle violated the Fourteenth Amendment.[64] The highest court validated the state statute without reference to the Fourteenth Amemdment, since the state statute did not bar use of weapons for self-defense. The 1968 decision of Duncan v. Louisiana[65] includes the concurring opinion of

Justice Black, and that opinion is frequently cited by these same zealots because the distinguished jurist had unwittingly recalled the words of a U.S. Senator in an 1866 congressional debate about the personal rights guaranteed and secured by the first eight amendments of the Constitution. "The right to keep and bear arms . . . the object of the first section . . . [being] to restrain the power of the states and compel them at all times to respect this great fundamental guarantee."[66] It was no matter that Duncan v. Louisiana was overruled in 1937 by Palko v. Connecticut;[67] the zealots deemed the 1937 decision of the highest court as marking "the point at which the Court first discredited and implicitly overruled Reconstruction-era cases which had held that the Due Process Clause of the Fourteenth Amendment did not apply the guarantees of the Bill of Rights to the States."[68] The highest court there observed: "Immunities that are valid as against the federal government by force of the specific pledges of particular amendments have been found to be implicit in the concept of ordered liberty, and thus, through the Fourteenth Amendment, become valid as against the States."[69] It is incredible that these zealots could compare the right to keep and bear arms with the "concept of ordered liberty," much less argue that the Second Amendment delineates "immunities that are valid as against the federal government," the very antithesis of the Second Amendment. The Palko case[70] involved the Fifth Amendment privilege against double jeopardy which was found *not* "implicit in the concept of ordered liberty," so that its denial by the state of Connecticut did not abridge Due Process of Law.

On May 29, 1940 the U.S. Department of Justice had announced that Attorney General Robert H. Jackson (later Associate Justice of the U.S. Supreme Court) had recommended to the Congress the enactment of a law which would require the registration of all firearms.[71] That recommendation was contained in a letter to William B. Bankhead, Speaker of the House of Representatives, as excerpted:

"My Dear Mr. Speaker:

I desire to recommend legislation to require registration of all firearms in the United States and a record of their transfers, accompanied by the imposition of a nominal tax on each transfer. Such a step would be of great importance in the interests of national defense, as it would hamper the possible accumulation of firearms on the part of subversive groups. It is also of outstanding importance in the enforcement of the criminal law.

It is only too well known to require detail depicting that federal, State and local law enforcement officers have frequently been killed by desperate criminals who equip themselves with firearms and have no hesitancy to use them in an endeavor to escape apprehension. On a number of occasions in recent years members of the personnel of the Federal Bureau of Investigation met their death in this manner while unflinchingly performing their hazardous duties. . . .

(The proposed legislation) would interfere with personal liberty no more than is the case with the requirement that is imposed in every State in respect to registration of automobiles. It is equally important that death-dealing weapons be registered so that a record of the traffic in them may be maintained for purposes of national defense and for enforcement of the criminal law.

(Note that) the provisions of the National Firearms Act, which was a registration and tax law enacted as one of the Crime Laws of the 73rd Congress apply only to certain types of weapons, including machine guns, submachine guns, sawed-off rifles and silencers. The Attorney General's recommendation would extend the registration and nominal tax provisions of the 1934 statute to all types of firearms.''

NOTES

1. Dred Scott v. Sandford, 60 US (19 How) 393 (1857).
2. 92 US 542 (1876).
3. Id. at p. 553.
4. Id.
5. See Hamline L Rev 69 (1974) at p. 73.
6. See Section 3 of Chapter 3.
7. See Halbrook, That Every Man Be Armed: The Evolution of a Constitutional Right (1984) at p. 159.
8. 116 US 252 (1886).
9. Id. at p. 265: ''It is undoubtedly true that all citizens capable of bearing arms constitute the reserved military force or reserve militia of the United States as well as of the States, and in view of this prerogative of the general government, as well as of its general powers, the States cannot, even laying the constitutional provision in question out of view, prohibit the people from keeping and bearing arms, so as to deprive the United States of their rightful resource of maintaining the public security and disable the people from performing their duty to the general government.''
10. Id. at p. 266.
11. Id. at p. 267.

12. Infra note 44 of chapter 3 at p. 167.
13. 153 US 535 (1894).
14. See 82 Mich L Rev 204 (Nov. 1983) at p. 247, footnote 183.
15. Infra note 13.
16. Id. at p. 538.
17. Id.
18. 165 US 275 (1897).
19. Id. at pp. 281-282.
20. 307 US 174 (1939).
21. 48 Stat 1237, 26 USC 5801-5872 (1982).
22. Infra note 18 at p. 178.
23. See 5 Fordham Urban L J (Fall 1976): "The Court did not benefit from the vigorous presentation of conflicting views which is considered a basic advantage of our adversary system of justice. The case was argued solely by the government attorneys who failed to alert the Court to the existence of several holdings clearly in favor of the individual's right to keep and bear arms."
24. 131 F2d 916 (lst Cir., 1942), rev'd on other grounds, 319 US 770 (1943) sub nom Cases Velasquez v. United States.
25. Id.; note that rehearing was denied 324 US 889 (1945).
26. Id.
27. Infra note 24.
28. 407 US 143 (1972) at p. 160.
29. 445 US 95 (1980).
30. See footnote 8 of the court's opinion.
31. 695 F2d 261 (7th Cir., 1982), cert den 104 S Ct 194 (1983).
32. 532 F Supp 1169 (ND Ill., 1981).
33. See 9 Hamline L Rev 69 (1974) at p. 76.
34. See Freedman, The Right of Privacy in the Computer Age (Quorum Books, 1987).
35. Infra note 31 at pp. 279-280.
36. 545 F2d 764 (lst Cir., 1976).
37. 477 F2d 610 (3rd Cir., 1973).
38. 497 F2d 548 (4th Cir., 1974).
39. 507 F2d 1034 (5th Cir., 1975).
40. 440 F2d 144 (6th Cir., 1971).
41. 444 F2d 1037 (7th Cir., 1971).
42. 438 F2d 764 (8th Cir., 1971).
43. 454 F2d 175 (9th Cir., 1972).
44. 564 F2d 384 (10th Cir., 1977).
45. Infra note 8 at p. 179.
46. 42 Tex 455 (1875).
47. 180 Col 20, 501 P2d 744 (1972).

48. 409 Ill 419, 94 NE2d 320 (1950).
49. 289 Ore 359, 614 P2d 94 (1980).
50. 398 NE2d 1339 (Ind App., 1980).
51. 523 SW2d 148 (Mo App., 1975).
52. 343 NE2d 847 (Mass., 1976).
53. 72 Kan. 230, 83 P 619 (1905).
54. Infra note 31.
55. 92 US 542 (1875).
56. 116 US 252 (1886).
57. See generally 2 Hastings Const L Q (Winter 1975).
58. Infra note 7.
59. 1 Ga 243 (1846).
60. Id. at p. 251.
61. 4 Ga 72 (1848).
62. 53 Ga 472 (1874).
63. Infra note 10 at p. 127.
64. 232 US 138 (1914).
65. 391 US 145 (1968).
66. Note Black, "The Bill of Rights," 35 NYU L Rev 865 (1960).
67. 302 US 319 (1937).
68. See 10 No Ky L Rev 63 (1962) by the assistant general counsel for the National Rifle Association in which he cites such cases as Hurtado v. California, 110 US 516 (1884), where the Fifth Amendment was not applied, and Walker v. Sauvinet, 92 US 90 (1875), where the Seventh Amendment was not applied.
69. Infra note 67 at pp. 324-325.
70. Id.
71. See New York Times (April 31, 1989) at A31.

5

Limitations on the Privilege to Keep and Bear Arms

5.1 POLICE POWER

Limitations on the privilege to keep and bear arms stem from the police power of state and local governments whose responsibilities include the making of reasonable regulations for protecting the health, safety, and welfare of the people. State constitutions implement this state police power, for example, by outlawing the presence of an armed body of men,[1] by proscribing concealed weapons carrying,[2] by regulating the manner of bearing arms,[3] and even by allowing minimum sentences for crimes committed while in the possession of a firearm.[4] In the exercise of police power pursuant to statute, for example, "the statute must reasonably tend to correct some evil or promote some interest of the State and not violate some positive mandate of the constitution."[5] Clearly the state legislature cannot nullify a federal or state constitutional provision or even supersede it.[6] As Tucker expressed it in 1899, "Constitutions are not made to create rights in the people, but in recognition of, and in order to preserve them, and that if any are specially enumerated and specially guarded, it is only because they are peculiarly important or peculiarly exposed to invasion."[7] A fitting example is found in the Pennsylvania Constitution of 1776, which recognized that "the inhabitants shall have liberty to fowl and hunt in seasonable times on the lands they hold, and on all other lands therein not inclosed."[8] The *Pennsylvania Evening Post* commented that under British hunting acts the "possession of hunting dogs, snares, nets, and other engines by unprivileged persons had been forbidden, and under pretense of last words, guns had been seized. And although this is not legal, as guns are not engines appropriate to kill game, yet if a witness can be found to attest before a Justice that a gun has thus been used, the penalty is five pounds or three months' imprisonment."[9] Police power recognizes the limitations on the privilege to keep and bear arms under constitutions and state laws.

American Rifleman Magazine (August 1985), a pro-gun publication, has pointed out that a survey of imprisoned felons "shows clearly that gun laws affect only the law-abiding and that criminals know it."[10] In short, the thrust is that police power should not embrace gun control, for law-abiding citizens are the only persons affected thereby. On the other hand, if law-abiding citizens are protected in their right to keep and bear arms, asserts the publication, criminals are "not going to mess around with a victim he knows is armed with a gun!" But how did the criminal get the gun in the first place? The survey intimates that criminals do not have easy access to guns: "criminals surveyed were often unarmed, 54% in Oklahoma, 62% in Georgia, 40% in Maryland, 43% in Missouri, and 35% in Florida."[11] But "the deterrent effect of citizen gun ownership" has lowered the crime rate. The publication states that "handguns are used for protection about 350,000 times each year in America," and this questionable statement means that the criminal was more often than not deterred or scared off from the commission of the crime because the "citizen gun owner" was armed and therefore "plays a significant proven role in curbing violent crime." An outright ban on handguns, according to the publication, "would have nightmarish consequences," for most criminals "would simply move to long guns which would be sawed down to concealable size. Outlawing handguns would simply make career criminals turn to . . . bigger, more lethal weapons."

No mention is made in the publication of who manufactures and distributes handguns for a profit. And, while handgun manufacturers and distributors would undoubtedly prefer a sale of a million handguns only to law-abiding citizens, the market for that much volume simply does not exist unless criminals are also permitted to enter the same market and purchase those handguns for their criminal purposes. Unless and until manufacturers and distributors of all guns are banned from the marketplace, criminals and crime rates will continue to soar due to the availability for a price of all sorts of guns. Gun control laws are but a step in the right direction until the people are sufficiently aroused to ban all guns from the marketplace. There is no reasons for citizens to turn to firearms for self-protection if criminals cannot have access to guns and the police power of the states is given supportive treatment.[12]

5.2 INDIVIDUAL RIGHT VERSUS COLLECTIVE RIGHT

The Second Amendment, "a well-regulated militia, being necessary to the security of a free state, the right of the people to keep and bear arms shall not be infringed," would appear to be clear and nonprovocative in meaning. But pro-gun zealots read into this one-sentence declaration a right protecting individual citizens in the peaceful ownership of private firearms for private purposes.[13] The anti-gun forces accept the literal meaning of the one-sentence declaration, a collective or corporate right approach, that the right runs only in favor of state governments and protects only state formal, organized militia units such as the National Guard.[14] A third or hybrid approach contends that the protected right is one for individual citizens but applies only to the ownership and use of firearms suitable for militia or military purposes of the State.[15]

The individual right to keep and bear arms has not met with judicial approval as perhaps best stated by the federal district court in Eckert v. Pennsylvania, where the plaintiff sought to enjoin the enforcement of the Pennsylvania Uniform Firearms Act.[16] He contended that this act infringed on his right to keep and bear arms under the Second Amendment: "The Supreme Court of the United States has held that the Second Amendment was not adopted to guarantee the right of the individual to bear arms, but rather to protect States 'in the maintenance of their militia organizations against possible encroachments by the federal power'."[17] Thus, unless the individual possession of arms bears a reasonable relationship to the preservation or efficiency of a well-regulated militia, there is no Second Amendment right to such possession, according to the court. A similar view was taken by the Tenth U.S. Court of Appeals in United States v. Swinton.[18] The defendant was convicted of engaging without a license in the business of selling firearms: "There is no absolute constitutional right of an individual to possess a firearm."[19]

The Sixth U.S. Court of Appeals the following year in United States v. Warin[20] stated that "the Second Amendment guarantees a collective rather than an individual right."[21] In 1982 the federal district court in Utah in Thompson v. Dereta[22] swung the cudgel with an emphatic statement that "the court is unaware of a single case which has upheld a right to bear arms under the Second Amendment to the Constitution, outside of the context of a militia."[23] All in all, there can be no violation of the Second Amendment unless the prohibited activity bears some reasonable relationship to the preservation or efficiency of a well-regulated militia.[24]

Even a state constitutional provision on the right to keep and bear arms will uphold the collective right view as seen in City of Salina v. Blaksley.[25] The Kansas constitution declared that "the people have a right to bear arms for their defense and security," and this provision, according to the Kansas Supreme Court, "refers to the people as a collective body. . . . Individual rights are not considered in this section." It should be observed that the 1986 *Harvard Journal of Law & Public Policy* did not agree with this approach.[26]

In 1982 the Utah Supreme Court in State v. Vlacil[27] interpreted the Second Amendment as providing a "collective" right to keep and bear arms, relying expressly upon the 1939 U.S. Supreme Court decision of United States v. Miller.[28] The Utah court justified a Utah state statute that prohibited aliens from possessing firearms as a valid exercise of State police power.[29] Strange as it may seem, the people of Utah were apparently unhappy with this "collective right" interpretation of the Utah constitution, which read, "The people have the right to bear arms for their security and defense, but the Legislature may regulate the exercise of this right by law."[30]

5.3 STATES' RIGHTS AND THE SECOND AMENDMENT

The Second Amendment in all its simplicity does not apply to states as has repeatedly been stated by the U.S. Supreme Court.[31] The Fourteenth Amendment does not cause the Second Amendment to be applied to the states.[32] However, state courts "at all levels, not the federal courts, . . . finally determine the overwhelming number of the vital issues of life, liberty and property that trouble countless human beings of this Nation every year."[33] Indeed, states have readily enacted gun control legislation under the collective right approach,[34] including the NRA-drafted Uniform Revolver Act, which served as basic handgun legislation for the several states.[35] The act included a prohibition on carrying concealed weapons as well as restrictions on gun ownership by felons, minors, and incompetents. State courts, for the most part, have rejected claims that state legislation restricting the possession of firearms violates state constitutional provisions.[36]

States' rights may evolve around the concept that the right to keep and bear arms is merely the protection of a "property right," which means that the state government need not protect property in absolute terms, but must, if the property is taken, provide reasonable compensation under due process of law.[37] The point is that the right to keep and bear arms is not a primary right like freedom of speech that must be protected at all cost. It may be nothing more than a matter of priorities, but the states have been content to legislate control over the "property" of the firearms, even though possession of arms is admittedly not valued as an end in itself. Self-defense and security of person, home, and property are the primary rights, but these ends can be achieved without dependence upon the possession of a gun.

5.4 "FOR PURPOSE OF SECURITY AND DEFENSE"

The obvious limitations on the privilege to keep and bear arms under the Second Amendment are further amplified by reference to what is meant by "security" and "defense." Historically the important item of "security" embraced security against foreign invasion, security against tyranny by the national as opposed to local government, security against oppression by local government, and security against crime. "Defense" is said to include defense of the state and self-defense.

Security against foreign invasion does not in the modern era require or mandate Second Amendment protection to gun owners. The military forces of the United States supply the arms, and private possession of arms is entirely unnecessary. A standing army and organized state militias are essential to assure security against foreign invasion.

Security against oppression by the federal government does not call for individual ownership of guns; indeed, individual ownership of firearms is irrelevant to protect against federal oppression. The U.S. Constitution itself is a "weapon" forged over the years to preclude federal (and state) oppression. The right of revolution does not mandate ownership of firearms by individuals; private arms ownership adds nothing to the balance of federal and state or local power. Security against oppression by state or local government follows the same pattern, and individual ownership of firearms should play no role whatsoever.

Security against crime opens the door to the issue of self-defense, especially where the crime may be directed toward the individual. But the police power of the jurisdiction must be the prime response to crime, not the individual "taking the law into his own hands," except possibly in matters of self-defense.[38] The opposing view is that private firearms ownership contributes to security against crime, even if the gun ownership is licensed and regulated.[39] Defense of home, person, and property means that people may use arms; but under the language of the Second Amendment only those arms suitable for militia use are protected.[40] Again police power is the more sensible "defense" so that there is full control over the use of arms. Concealed-weapons carrying is a vice that mandates policing as do terroristic threats involving the use of firearms.[41]

A 1986 decision of the Maine Supreme Court upheld the illegal possession of firearms conviction of a felon who argued that he had a constitutional right to bear arms; the court ruled that Maine residents had that right only "for the common defense".[42] In the belief that this conclusion threatened the sale of guns in Maine, the legislature voted to delete the words from the Maine Constitution.

NOTES

1. See Wash. Const., Article I, Section 24, for example.
2. See Colo. Const., Article II, Section 13, for example.
3. See Fla. Const., Article I, Section 8, for example.
4. See Idaho Const., Article I, Section 11, for example.
5. People v. Warren, 11 Ill2d 420, 143 NE2d 28 (1957) at pp. 424 and 31. Also see 7 Okla City U L Rev (1982) at p. 185.
6. See Junction City v. Mevis, 226 Kan. 526, 601 P2d 1145 (1979), voiding the gun ordinance.
7. 2 Tucker, The Constitution of the U.S. 688 (1899).
8. See 7 Thorpe, The Federal and State Constitutions (1909) at p. 3091.
9. Id.
10. At pp. 1 et seq.
11. Id.
12. See Draper, Preface to The Issue of Gun control at pp. 5-6. (T. Draper, ed., 1981). The author states:

The pro-control argument is that some kind of regulation of the private possession of handguns—the weapons most adaptable to close-range bodily assault—will result in fewer crimes and less human destruction. Of those opposed to regulation, some fear that it would lead inevitably first to a ban on hunting rifles and shotguns and then to other encroachments on human freedom. Others argue that while the handgun is the cheapest and most versatile firearm for use in crime, it is also the most practical means of personal protection *against* crime. In this survey of current opinion on the issue of gun control, no disagreement was found on the need to stem the increasing volume of handgun violence and also to keep down the rising number of Saturday Night Specials in society. (Most estimates of the number of firearms in private hands [in the United States] . . . range from 140 million to 200 million.) Where disagreement begins is over evaluation of evidence found in books, articles, congressional hearings, and studies to support the contention that fewer handguns would indeed mean fewer crimes. . . ."

See generally 31 Villanova L Rev 1577 (1986); also Turley & Harrison, "*Strict Tort Liability of Handgun Suppliers,*" 6 Hamline L Rev 285 (1983):

"Every thirteen seconds a new handgun is sold in this country, every two and a half minutes the product injures someone and three times every hour it is an instrument of death. The handgun is ranked second only to motor vehicles as the cause of unnatural deaths in this country. There are an estimated fifty million handguns in the United States today . . . [and] two and [a] half million [are] sold each year. . . . the result is some twenty-two thousand handgun deaths annually in this country alone." (at 285-286), citing U.S. Dep't of Justice, F.B.I. Uniform Crime Reports 130 (1980); 2 Mortality Statistics Branch, Division of Vital Statistics, Vital Statistics of the United States 23 (1981); Bureau of Alcohol, Tobacco and Firearm Statistics (1980); U.S. Dep't of Justice, Report of the U.S. Attorney General's Task Force on Violent Crime (1979).

13. See 5 Fordham Urban L J 31 (1976) for example.
14. See 48 Chi-Kent L Rev 148 (1971).
15. See United States v. Miller, 307 US 174 (1939) relating to the possession of an unregistered sawed-off shotgun.
16. 331 F Supp 1361 (ED Pa., 1971).
17. Id. at p. 1362.
18. 521 F2d 1255 (10th Cir., 1975).
19. Id. at p. 1259.
20. 530 F2d 103 (6th Cir., 1976).
21. Id. at p. 106.
22. 549 F Supp 297 (Utah, 1982).
23. Id. at p. 299.
24. Also note Englom v. Carey, 522 F Supp 57 (SDNY, 1981).
25. 72 Kan. 230, 83 P 619 (1905).
26. 9 Harv J of Law & Pub Pol 632 (1986).
27. 645 P2d 677 (Utah, 1982).
28. 307 US 174 (1939).
29. Utah Code Ann. (76-10-503(1) (1978) provides in part: "Any person who is not a citizen of the United States . . . shall not own or have in his

possession or under his custody or control any dangerous weapon as defined in this part. Any person who violates this section is guilty of a class A misdemeanor, and if the dangerous weapon is a firearm or sawed-off shotgun he shall be guilty of a felony of the third degree.''

30. See 1986 Utah L Rev 751 (1986) at p. 752.

31. See Miller v. Texas, 153 US 535 (1894) and cases cited in Section 1 of Chapter 4.

32. See Section 4 of Chapter 4.

33. See Brennan, ''Introduction: Chief Justice Hughes and Justice Mountain,'' 10 Seton Hall L Rev xii (1979).

34. See 82 Mich L Rev 204 (Nov. 1983) at pp. 211 et seq.

35. Id. at p. 210.

36. Note 7 Okla L Rev 177 (1982) at pp. 186-191.

37. See Stackhouse, Creeds, Society and Human Rights: A Study in Three Cultures (1984).

38. See Section 1 of this chapter.

39. See 9 Hamline L Rev 69 (1974) at p. 99.

40. See Ex Parte Thomas, 97 P 260 (Okla. Crim., 1908).

41. See State v. Hogan, 63 Ohio St 202, 58 NE 572 (1900):

> The constitutional right to bear arms is intended to guaranty to the people, in support of just government, such right, and to afford the citizen means for defense of self and property. While this secures to him a right of which he cannot be deprived, it enjoins the duty in execution of which that right is to be exercised. If he employs those arms which he ought to wield for the safety and protection of his country, his person and his property, to the annoyance and terror and danger of its citizens, his acts find no vindication in the bill of rights. That guaranty was never intended as a warrant for vicious persons to carry weapons with which to terrorize others. Going armed with unusual and dangerous weapons, to the terror of the people, is an offense at common law. A man may carry a gun for any lawful purpose, for business or amusement, but he cannot go about with that or any other dangerous weapon to terrify and alarm a peaceful people.

42. See the Hartford Courant (November 1, 1987) at p. AA1.

6

Firearm and Gun Control Legislation

6.1 INTRODUCTION

The Second Amendment comes into play as the federal, state, and local governments endeavor to exercise jurisdiction over "arms" in all shapes and sizes. The validity of firearms and gun control legislation is measured by numerous federal and state constitutional requirements such as Equal Protection of the Law,[1] Due Process of Law,[2] and Privilege Against Self-Incrimination,[3] among others. Courts have apparently been reluctant to strike down such statutes and ordinances on keeping and bearing arms as attested to by the relatively few statutes and ordinances voided over the years.[4] It is estimated that there are more than 20,000 federal, state, and local gun control laws.[5]

Among the important questions raised with respect to the validity of gun control laws are those pertaining to the powers of Congress under the Interstate Commerce Clause to control or even ban the manufacture of guns for sale in interstate commerce. In Scarborough v. United States the U.S. Supreme Court in 1977 declared that the Commerce Clause extends to the prohibition of possession of any firearm which has at any time traveled in interstate or foreign commerce.[6] But such a pervasive prohibition might run afoul of the Third and Fourth Amendments because a citizen has a right to protect his home or "castle," as delineated in Stanley v. Georgia, decided by the U.S. Supreme Court in 1969.[7] In that case the Court barred legislation prohibiting the possession of pornography in the home. Confiscation of firearms and guns would violate the Fifth Amendment unless the compensation was fair and just and the "taking" was for public use.[8]

6.2 FEDERAL STATUTES ON GUN CONTROL

The first federal gun control laws were enacted in the 1920s and in the 1930s and served as the only federal firearms legislation until the 1960s. Then, in response to the assassination of prominent political figures, the Gun Control Act of 1968 was enacted.[9] This act abrogated the older legislation and focused on the issue of preventing crime by limiting public access to firearms and guns. In Huddleston v. United States the U.S. Supreme Court stated clearly that the purpose of the Gun Control Act of 1968 was to curb crime by keeping "firearms out of the hands of those not legally entitled to possess them because of age, criminal background or incompetency."[10]

Just thirty years earlier Congress had enacted the National Firearms Act of 1934, which was aimed squarely at machine guns and similar offensive weapons.[11] On May 19, 1986, the Gun Control Act of 1968[12] was amended by the enactment of the Firearms Owners' Protection Act[13] and effective November 15, 1986, by the McClure-Volkmer Amendments.[14] A review of the Federal Gun Control Act of 1968 as amended is therefore in order.

The act generally prohibits sale of firearms to certain classes of person ranging from felons[15] to those who have renounced citizenship or are users of marijuana.[16] Interstate transport of firearms is strictly limited, mail-order sales are abolished, and sales to out-of-state residents are with minor exceptions made criminal.[17] A firearms dealer is required to verify the identity and residence of a buyer and to record the identity as well as the firearms or ammunition sold. All records are open to inspection by the Bureau of Alcohol, Tobacco and Firearms (BATF) of the U.S. Department of the Treasury. The centerpiece of the act is to control illicit traffic in firearms, as purchasers of firearms must meet minimum federal standards as well as state and local regulations. Section 927 of 18 U.S. Code for example, provides that Congress does not intend to preempt state firearms law unless the particular state and federal provisions directly conflict and cannot be reconciled. Under Sections 922(a)(1) and 923(a) it is unlawful for anyone except a licensed dealer to engage in the business of dealing in firearms or ammunition. In

United States v. Brooks[18] the Fifth U.S. Court of Appeals affirmed the guilt of the defendant dealer under 18 USC 922(b)(3)(m) because he knowingly sold firearms to a person whom he knew or should have known to be a nonresident. In other words, the person who pays for the firearms and to whom the defendant knowingly transfered possession and control of the firearms was a nonresident alien.[19] Any firearm or ammunition involved in, used in, or intended to be used in violation of the act or any other federal criminal law is subject to seizure and forfeiture.[20]

The McClure-Volkmer Amendments to the Federal Gun Control Act of 1968 became effective on November 15, 1986. Among the numerous provisions are that (1) non-licensees may buy rifles and shotguns from licensed dealers in other states as long as the transaction is lawful in both the buyer's state of residence and the dealer's state of business; (2) any legally owned firearm may be transported through a state or jurisdiction that otherwise might make such a transaction illegal, provided the transaction is lawful in the state of destination of the firearm; (3) all persons barred from receiving firearms may seek relief from the disability, including felons whose crimes involved using a firearm; (4) forfeiture of firearms is limited to those specific firearms and ammunition "involved in or used in" or "intended to be used in" specified offenses "where such intent is demonstrated by clear and convincing evidence"; and forfeiture proceedings must be commenced within 120 days of seizure;[21] (5) BATF is restricted to one unannounced compliance inspection of records and inventory within any twelve month period of time; all government inspections require a warrant except in the course of a criminal investigation of a person other than the licensee or for tracing firearms; (6) sales of machine guns manufactured after May 19, 1986, are banned other than to government agencies; (7) the requirement that dealers in ammunition obtain a license is deleted; (8) record-keeping requirements for dealers in firearms is reduced; and (9) a mandatory prison term of five years for any person who uses or carries a firearm during and in relation to a drug trafficking offense is established.[22]

The Firearms Owners' Protection Act (FOPA)[23] was the first comprehensive redraft of the federal firearm laws since 1968.[24] Passage of this legislation took seven years in Congress because it overruled, effective May 19, 1986, six decisions of the U.S. Supreme Court and negated perhaps one third of the total case law construing the Gun Control Act of 1968.[25] By expressly exempting interstate transportation of firearms from the reach of many state firearm laws, FOPA also affected state proceedings. FOPA reflects a series of legislative compromises making the statute unclear and even ambiguous in many particulars. Some of its vital provisions are: (1) a dealer's license is required to deal in firearms business;[26] (2) sales to nonresidents are permitted unless the sale would be "in violation of any published ordinance or law of the state or locality where such person resides";[27] (3) there is a listing of prohibited buyers of firearms; (4) criminal prosecution for proof of willful violation; and (5) any state law or regulation prohibiting transfer of a firearm in interstate commerce through the state is null and void, provided the firearm is unloaded and not readily accessible.[28]

The first American handgun ban was enacted in the year 1837[29] and restrictions on the sale or carrying of handguns have been commonplace ever since.[30] The sole federal statute banning handguns was the 1927 ban on the use of the mails to ship firearms concealable on one's person.[31] In 1988 advocates of gun control sought to require a seven-day waiting period for the sale of gun purchases, but by a vote of 228-182 the U.S. House of Representatives defeated the measure which would have been part of a major drug enforcement bill.[32] It should be noted that the nation's law enforcement officials, as a united group, had unsuccessfully lobbied in favor of the waiting period which is already the law in 22 states.[33] The provision would have required the applicant-purchaser of a gun or pistol to wait a week so that police could investigate whether the purchaser was a felon, an illegal alien, a drug abuser, or mentally ill. According to the *New York Times* (September 16, 1988), "in the gun control debate both sides agreed with a federal survey indicating that only about 20% of the guns used by criminals are purchased legally in gun shops."[34] Expensive lobbying was said to have paid off for the National Rifle Association and its satellite organizations: "Although the rifle association outspent the largest gun control group by a margin of more than 7 to 1 in contributions, the people interviewed said . . . that the group's real power came from the intensive lobbying drive that cost nearly $3 million. The rifle association mailed as many as three letters to each of its 2.8 million members, alerting them that legislation proposing a seven-day waiting period for buying a pistol would seriously infringe on their right to bear arms. Many members, heeding advice in those letters, wrote, telephoned, and in some cases buttonholed their representatives, imploring them to vigorously oppose the legislation."[35] And "nine of every ten House members who collected contributions from the National Rifle Association from January 1, 1987 to June 30, 1988 voted in favor of the substitute (anti-waiting period) bill.''[36] The average NRA contribution to each House member voting with the National Rifle Association was $1,964.[37]

Another federal statute, the Federal Hazardous Substances Act[38] was involved in Committee for Hand Gun Control, Inc. v. Consumer Product Safety Commission.[39] The Consumer Product Safety Commission (CPSC) was deemed to have the authority, power, and jurisdiction under the act to promulgate a regulation banning the manufacture, sale, and distribution of handgun ammunition in interstate commerce, with the exception of use by military, police, security guards, and gun clubs.[40]

6.3 STATE STATUTES ON GUN CONTROL

An elementary question might be raised at the outset: since there are federal laws regulating firearms and guns, why are state and local laws necessary? Supporters of federal control contend that state laws are too often ineffective because they are easily evaded by simply crossing a state line. The primary thrust of federal laws is the interstate ''leakage'' of firearms and guns. But the issue of states' rights includes such questions as why states should not have as much autonomy as possible in drafting their criminal laws and enforcing their statutes. Indeed, nothing at the federal level corresponds to a street police force and local police agencies where most law enforcement personnel are concentrated. On the other hand, the need for gun control does differ from state to state; some states have limited crime, while other states are overwhelmed with violent crime.[41]

Firearm and gun control statutes, whether federal or state or local, have generally been upheld as constitutional and not in conflict with the Second Amendment. United States v. Turcotte upheld conviction for false written statements in connection with the purchase of a firearm.[42] In United States v. Three Winchester . . . Carbines[43] the federal district court upheld conviction of a felon for possession of firearms.[44] The Minnesota Supreme Court in 1980 in In Re Atkinson[45] declared: ''Whatever the scope of any common law or constitutional right to bear arms, we hold that it is not absolute and does not guarantee to individuals the right to carry loaded weapons abroad at all times and in all circumstances. . . . The State may reasonably exercise its police power to regulate the carrying of weapons by individuals in the interest of public safety. Exercise of the State's police power must be upheld unless it bears no relation to public health, safety, morals, or general welfare.''[46]

The landmark case of Quilici v. Village of Morton Grove reflects the view that a federal court may uphold the constitutionality of a village ordinance banning all handguns within the village except for handguns for police officers, members of the armed forces, and licensed gun owners.[47] The ground was the reasonable exercise of police power to protect public safety and public health, but the important implication was that the Second Amendment did *not* apply to the states.[48] The Seventh U.S. Court of Appeals observed that the Second Amendment made it abundantly ''clear that the right to bear arms is inextricably connected to the preservation of a militia,'' and therefore any private possession of arms is unprotected by the Second Amendment.[49] Earlier the New Jersey Supreme Court in Burton v. Sills had agreed that the Second Amendment would not be applied to the states through incorporation into the Due Process Clause of the Fourteenth Amendment.[50]

Gun permits or licenses to possess a gun are frequently the subject of litigation, as illustrated by the New York case of Birnbaum v. Ward.[51] Here the petitioner sought to vacate a decision by the city to revoke his gun permit, despite the fact that petitioner had apparently violated the rule that guns must be transported unloaded and in a locked container. The court upheld the decision of the city, since the penalty imposed was consistent with prior penalties imposed for this type of violation. In the same vein was Nowogrodzki v. Ward, which upheld the administrative determination that petitioner for a pistol permit had failed to make a prima facie showing of need in his gold jewelry business.[52] The petitioner had failed ''to show a need sufficient to distinguish himself from others who do business in New York City without the benefit of a license to carry a concealed weapon. . . . Petitioner has not demonstrated that he faces a danger substantially greater than others engaged in a similar business.'' Toy guns, which resemble the real thing, have been implicated in robberies and other crimes, so the state of New York in 1988 enacted special legislation that defined ''imitation weapons'' as any plastic, wood, or metal object which substantially duplicates or can reasonably be perceived to be an actual firearm.[53] But such an article is not considered to be an ''imitation weapon'' if it meets specified statutory criteria, i.e., the weapon is not black, blue, silver, or aluminum in color; it has at least a one-inch wide orange stripe down each side of its entire barrel and front, and has a closed barrel. Non-firing replicas of antique firearms are excluded, as are imitation guns used in theatrical productions.

The town of Kennesaw, Georgia, in April 1987 enacted an ordinance requiring every resident to keep a working firearm in the house along with a supply of ammunition for it.[54] The 8,500 residents thus took a counterproductive step to a safe society, but they were supported by Gun Owners of America, a 200,000-member group headquartered in Washington, D.C.[55] In Colorado, there is a state law authorizing residents to use "deadly force" against intruders in their home;[56] the law is popularly known as the "make my day" statute but bears the official name of Homeowner Protection Act of 1985.

The state of Florida has a constitutional provision that the right of citizens to keep and bear arms in self-defense and in defense of the state "shall not be infringed." But the constitutional provision[57] concludes that "the manner of bearing arms may be regulated by law."[58] The state had gone further in invoking state gun control by preempting counties and localities. But controversial issues still arise, and there has been polarization of proponents of strict gun control and supporters of an absolute constitutional right to keep and bear arms. One area of focus is whether liberal, concealed weapons laws deter crime, since criminals do not want to be shot any more than do noncriminals.[59] Another issue is whether allowing more citizens to carry weapons, especially in urban areas, will increase the number of gun-related offenses and the rate of violent crime. A majority of states have statutes prohibiting the carrying of concealed weapons.[60] Vermont, interestingly, makes it unlawful for a person to carry "a dangerous or deadly weapon, open or concealed, with the intent or avowed purpose of injuring a fellow man."[61]

The State of Maryland, in November 1988, in the first statewide referendum controlling guns, voted 58 percent in favor of controlling the sale of cheaply made and easily concealed weapons. The new law established a commission that will decide which handguns are appropriate for sport shooting and self-defense and which handguns are useful only for criminals.[62] But the commission does not begin its work until January 1, 1990. The Maryland referendum was clearly a vote for gun control, despite the onslaught of the National Rifle Association: "It is well known that the NRA poured $6.1 million into Maryland to overturn a State law banning cheap, concealable handguns. Voters nevertheless supported the legislation by a wide margin, as the NRA suffered its first defeat in a Statewide referendum on gun control.''[63]

6.4 THE NATURE OF THE STATUTE ON GUN CONTROL

Firearms and gun control statutes may be categorized according to such aspects as place and manner of use, ownership by certain persons, the nature and extent of the danger of the weapon, ammunition control, and licensing and registration. The place and manner in which the firearms may be carried is the subject of most statutes on firearms and gun control. Forbidden are such practices as carrying concealed weapons,[64] carrying pistols within the city,[65] bringing weapons into a courtroom,[66] or simply carrying of firearms off the owner's premises.[67]

Certain persons like felons and incompetents should not have access to firearms and guns, but this aspect of statutes on firearms and gun control appears to have no impact on deterrence nor on widespread possession of arms.[68] Furthermore, the right of self-defense should not be impaired.[69]

Unusually dangerous weapons should and are prohibited by statutes, for it is simply too dangerous to tolerate their use in a civilized community. In 1969 the National Commission on the Causes and Prevention of Violence recommended that the possession of handguns should be limited to ``police officers and security guards, small business in high crime areas, and others with special need for self- protection.''[70] Nevertheless, apparently no state has taken the cudgel and outlawed handguns for certain elements of the population, probably out of consideration of the Equal Protection of the Law Clause, although the constitutionality of such statutes would be upheld on the ground that the individuals in certain prescribed groups are more likely to misuse handguns than members of the population at large. As spelled out in Turner v. Fouche, the ``traditional test for a denial of equal protection is whether the challenged classification rests on grounds wholly irrelevant to the achievement of a valid State objective.''[71]

Some statutes seek to control the distribution of ammunition and not the firearms and guns, but the impact on deterrence is minimal.[72] These statutes are generally valid if ammunition for other firearms and guns is available.[73]

Statutes requiring licensing and registration usually support measures to insure that guns and firearms do not fall into the hands of those persons not entitled to possess them. Their validity is clear, although such statutes may be permissive or restrictively discretionary.[74] An example of the former statute is Section 29-33 of Connecticut General Statutes, which states that handguns may be purchased only upon application, which is deemed granted unless within two weeks the licensing authority rejects it, based upon a finding of a felony conviction, for example. Neither the permissive or restrictively discretionary statute per se violates the Second Amendment, since both types of statutes operate only to exclude firearms or gun ownership by those persons upon whom the Second Amendment confers no right or privilege.[75]

A prime factor in analyzing any statute for control of firearms and guns is a recognition that regulation of some kind is to be expected, and the person dealing in or buying guns and firearms is presumed to be aware of the law.[76] Knowledge is not necessary to uphold a conviction because of the inherent nature of the business of firearms and guns.[77]

6.5 SALES OF FIREARMS AND GUNS

According to *Insight* magazine (November 30, 1987), gun sales in the United States are generally on the increase. In 1981 there were 2,537,229 United States–manufactured handguns sold, the highest in the ten-year period from 1976 to 1986.[78] In 1985 only 1,550,071 United States–manufactured handguns were sold, but there was undoubtedly a hugh increase in foreign-manufactured handguns. The National Rifle Association with its 2.8 million members is opposed by the Handgun Control, Inc., lobby of 1 million members. It would appear that "the rate of gun ownership is greatest in the Southern and Mountain states and lowest in the Northeast and Pacific states. . . . Highly restrictive New York (apparently) ranks first among the states in robbery, though fairly unrestrictive Florida ranks second."[79] Prices for handguns start as low as $167.30 for plain, matte black .38 special revolver, which holds five rounds and has a two-inch or snub-nosed barrel. A 9mm handgun manufactured in Brazil sells for only $145. The handgun resale market is estimated to be $1.2 billion annually. The largest handgun manufacturers are Smith & Wesson, Sturm, Ruger & Co., and Colt Industries, Inc.[80]

The growth of violent crime committed with firearms is a subject of great concern to law enforcement officers in particular.[81] Countless research projects have fortified preexisting beliefs. One recent study, entitled "An Analysis of Law Enforcement Officer Attitudes Toward the Control of Handguns," lent credence and support to such regulatory methods of handgun control as "background investigations for prospective purchasers, time delays between the sale and actual receipt of a handgun, and programs which would require mandatory completion of a firearms safety course prior to purchasing a handgun."[82] But the revealing conclusion of this 1983 study was that "few of the respondent officers believed that current gun laws and their accompanying sanctions deter criminal offenders from either obtaining handguns or using them unlawfully."

NOTES

1. See State v. Krantz, 24 Wash. 2d 350, 164 P2d 453 (1945).

2. See Duncan v. Louisiana, 391 US 145 (1967).

3. See Marchetti v. United States, 390 US 39 (1968). See generally 38 U of Chi L Rev 185 (1970).

4. See State v. Blocker, 291 Ore. 255, 630 P.2d 824 (1981); State v. Kessler, 289 Ore. 359, 614 P.2d 94 (1980); Glasscock v. City of Chattanooga, 157 Tenn. 518, 11 S.W.2d 678 (1928); Andrews v. State, 50 Tenn. 165 (1871); Smith v. Ishenhour, 43 Tenn. 214, 217 (1966); Jennings v. State, 5 Tex. Crim. App. 298 (1878); State v. Rosenthal, 75 Vt. 295, 55 A. 610 (1903). Wilson v. State, 33 Ark. 557 (1878); City of Lakewood v. Pillow, 180 Colo. 20, 23 501 P.2d 744, 745 (1972) (en banc); People v. Nakamura, 99 Colo. 262, 62 P.2d 246 (1936) (en banc); Nunn v. State, 1 Ga. (1 Kelly) 243 (1846); *In re* Brickey, 8 Idaho 597, 70 P. 609 (1902); Bliss v. Commonwealth, 12 Ky. (2 Litt.) 90 (1822); People v. Zerillo, 219 Mich. 635, 189 N.W. 927 (1922); City of Las Vegas v. Moberg, 82 N.M. 626, 485 P.2d 737 (Ct. App. (1971); State v. Kerner, 181 N.C. 574, 107 S.E. 222 (1921); *In re* Reilly, 31 Ohio Dec. 364 (C.P. 1919).

5. See 82 Mich L Rev 204 (Nov. 1983) at p. 207.

6. 431 US 563 (1977).

7. 394 US 557 (1969).

8. See §1.6.

9. Pub Law No. 90-618, 82 Stat 1213, codified as amended at 18 USC 921-928 (1981):

> The GCA was enacted shortly after the assassination of Robert Kennedy and is in reality an intricate combination of coordinating provisions and amendments to existing laws. The GCA was passed as a compromise piece of legislation among the various pro- and

anti-gun factions. The primary focus of Title 1 of the GCA is to provide federal assistance to state firearms control efforts by requiring licensing for all persons dealing in firearms or ammunition. The GCA also specifies certain high risk individuals who are declared ineligible to purchase firearms. Other provisions in the Title prohibit interstate mail order sale of all firearms and ammunition, interstate sale of all handguns, interstate sale of certain long guns, and importation of nonsporting firearms.

The fundamental theory underlying these provisions was that by limiting the ease of obtaining firearms, guns would be less available to high risk individuals, thus resulting in a lower violent crime rate. By strict federal licensing of dealers and bans on interstate direct and mail-order sales, Congress intended to impose more stringent controls on the gun industry. In addition, by decreasing mail-order and interstate sales, the law sought to ensure that gun dealers knew the persons to whom they sold guns. To achieve those objectives, Congress imposed criminal penalties for the illegal sale and use of guns. Dealers who did not comply with the GCA could be held criminally liable and subject to jail terms or substantial fines, as well as confiscation of any weapons or ammunition held or possessed in violation of the Act. Furthermore, criminals who *used* a firearm in the commission of a crime faced penalties in addition to those imposed for the underlying substantive crime. An additional penalty was also imposed for the unlawful carrying of firearms during the commission of a crime.

The GCA attempted to balance a congressional desire to aid local law enforcement agencies in crime prevention; at the same time it attempted to avoid substantial restrictions on acquisition, possession, and use of firearms by law-abiding citizens. (6 Hamline L Rev 409 at pp. 410-411; footnotes omitted)

10. 415 US 815 (1974) at p. 822.

11. See 9 Harv J of L & Pub. Pol. 559 (1986).

12. 82 Stat 1213, codified at 18 USC 921-928 and 26 USC 5801, 5802, 5811, 5821, 5840-5849, 5871, 6808, and 7273 (1982).

13. Pub L 99-308 (1986). The Preamble begins, "The Congress finds that (1) the rights of citizens . . . (A) to keep and bear arms under the Second Amendment to the United States Constitution . . . require additional legislation to correct existing firearms statutes."

14. The 1986 amendment, 100 Stat 449, eff. May 19, 1986, is at 18 USC 921.

15. Under 18 USC 922(a)(5)(B) a gun may be loaned to a person in another state, or even rented, for "lawful sporting" purposes.

16. See 18 USC 922 (g)-(h); under 18 USC 922 (d)(1) licensed manufacturers, importers, dealers, or collectors are prohibited from transferring firearms to such persons.

17. Other provisions prohibit persons charged with assasination, kidnapping, or assault of a member of Congress (18 USC 351), persons charged with mutiny or riots at federal prisons, or the transportation into such institutions of firearms or other lethal weapons (18 USC 1792); persons charged with willful destruction of an aircraft or aircraft facilities or the willful incapacitation of an aircraft crew member (18 USC 32); persons charged with the willful destruction of a motor

vehicle or motor vehicle facilities or the incapacitation of a driver (18 USC 33), persons charged with threats to take the life of or inflict bodily harm on the president or successors to the presidency (18 USC 871); and persons charged with interference with foreign commerce by violence, through the use of fire or explosives (18 USC 1364).

18. *611* F2d *614* (5th Cir., 1980).

19. The official BATF interpretation (BATF 03310.4) of the sections read as follows:

Section 922(b)(3)

a. *Description*:
Licensed person selling or delivering firearm to an unlicensed person whom the licensee knows or has reasonable cause to believe does not reside in the State in which the licensee's place of business is located.

b. *Elements*:

(1) Accused is a licensee.
(2) Accused sold or delivered a firearm to another person.
(3) Purchaser was unlicensed. (Matter of affirmative defense.)
(4) Purchaser did not reside in State in which accused's place of business was located.
(5) Accused knew or had reasonable cause to believe that purchaser did not reside in State in which accused's place of business was located.
(6) Date of sale and/or delivery.
(7) Place of sale and/or delivery.
(8) Location of accused's place of business.
(9) If firearm was a rifle or shotgun and purchaser resided in State contiguous to State in which accused's place of business was location.
   (a) Purchaser's State of residence does not by law permit such sale or delivery.
   (b) The sale did not comply with legal conditions of sale in one or both contiguous States.
   (c) Purchaser and/or licensee did not, prior to the sale, or delivery for sale, of the rifle or shotgun, comply with all of the requirements of § 922(c) applicable to intrastate transactions other than at licensee's place of business.

Exceptions:

(1) Delivery of such firearm by the licensee was a loan or rental of a firearm to a person for temporary use for lawful sporting purposes.
(2) Firearm sold or delivered was a rifle or shotgun obtained by the purchaser to replace a firearm which was lost, stolen, or became inoperative while the purchaser was in the State of purchase participating in organized rifle or shotgun match or contest, or engaged in hunting, and purchaser did present to the licensee a sworn statement (1) concerning the loss, theft, or inoperative condition of the firearm replaced and showing that such purchaser was participating in an organized shooting match or contest or was engaged in hunting, and (2) identifying the chief law enforcement officer of the area where purchaser resides to whom licensee shall forward such sworn statement by registered mail.
(3) Accused was returning firearm or replacement firearm of the same kind and type to

a person from whom it was received. (Matter of affirmative defense—exception appears in § 922(a)(2)(A).)

20. 18 USC 924(d).

21. Should the gun owner prevail, the court shall award an attorney's fee and return the property.

22. The 1986 amendments, according to House Report No. 99-495, were "to relieve the nation's sportsmen and firearms owners and dealers from unnecessary burdens under the Federal Gun Control Act of 1968."

23. Infra note 10.

24. See generally 11 Cumberland L Rev 585 (1987).

25. Id. at pp. 586-587.

26. Apparently there are four elements that must be proven to establish "engaging in the business of" dealing in firearms: devotion of time, attention and labor to such dealing; as a regular course of trade or business; with the principal objective of livelihood and profit; and through the repetitive purchase and resale of firearms.

27. FOPA does not define residency, although generally a person is a resident of the locale where he is permanently or for substantial period of time physically located.

28. Infra note 24.

29. Act of December 25, 1837, Digest of the Statute Laws of the State of Georgia in Effect Prior to the Session of the General Assembly of 1851, at 818 (1851). See Nunn v. State, 1 Ga. 243 (1846).

30. Act of March 18, 1889, 1889 Ariz. Sess Laws 16.

31. See 18 USC 1715 (1982).

32. See New York Times (September 16, 1988) at A13. The House substituted a provision designed to give drug dealers quick access to criminal records so as to identify felons trying to buy firearms.

33. Id.

34. At A13.

35. See New York Times (September 22, 1988) at A32.

36. Id.

37. Note opening paragraph of the New York Times (September 7, 1988) editorial at A30:

> How can you attack Michael Dukakis as soft on crime, Dan Quayle's news conference questioner wanted to know, when you oppose Federal laws to prevent a convict from walking into a store and buying a gun? "They can't just walk into a store and buy a gun," the Republican Vice Presidential candidate replied. "There are all sorts of restrictions." He was wrong. In many parts of America, no one checks to see if gun customers have criminal or psychiatric records. But the mistake suggests that even a committed foe of gun control like Mr. Quayle accepts the rationale behind an important proposal for new gun regulation.

38. 18 USC 1261 et seq., 74 Stat 372.
39. 388 F Supp 216 (D.C., 1974).
40. The following is an excerpt of the court decision:

Under the Act a "hazardous substance" means, *inter alia,* "[a]ny substance or mixture of substances which . . . (v) is flammable or combustible, or (vi) generates pressure through decomposition, heat, or other means, if such substance or mixture of substances may cause substantial personal injury or substantial illness during or as a proximate result of any customary or reasonably foreseeable handling or use, including reasonably foreseeable ingestion by children." 15 U.S.C. § 1261(f)(1)(A). The administrator of the Act, originally the Secretary of Health, Education and Welfare, but now the CPSC, has authority to determine by regulation which susbtances meet the definition of "hazardous substance." Id. §1262. If a substance is determined to be hazardous, the administrator may decide to exempt it from the Act's requirements, may require labeling, or may ban it from interstate commerce. . . . If the CPSC, after full consideration of plaintiff's petition, should conclude that access to handgun ammunition must be restricted, that does not appear at odds with any Congressional intent expressed with regards to the FHSA. That Congressional intent expressed in barring CPSC consideration of guns and ammunition as a "consumer product" under the CPSA [Consumer Product Safety Act], is not the type of clear legislative history regarding a totally separate Act which would allow the court to deviate from the plain and literal meaning of the statute. If the Commission remains convinced that Congress would object to the CPSC giving consideration to the merits of plaintiff's petition, the proper course is for the Commission to seek clarification from Congress. Absent such clarification, however, and given the clear and unrestricted language of the FHSA [Federal Hazardous Substances Act], the 13-year history of exercising jurisdiction over small-arms ammunition, and the broad view of jurisdiction generally given the FHSA, . . . the CPSC has jurisdiction to consider plaintiff's petition. Accordingly, an appropriate declaratory judgment shall issue.

41. In 1981 South Dakota had only 12 murders and nonnegligent manslaughters and 122 robberies,while Nevada with only 23 percent more inhabitants had 148 homicides and 3,867 robberies. See generally 49 Law & Contem Prob 1 (Winter 1986).
42. See 18 USC 922.
43. 363 F Supp 322 (ED Wis., 1973).
44. See 18 USC 1202A.
45. 256 NW2d 298 (Minn., 1980).
46. Id. at pp. 302-304; also see Section 1 of chapter 4.
47. 532 F Supp 1169 (ND Ill., 1981), aff 695 F2d 261 (7th Cir., 1982).
48. Id. at p. 270.
49. Id. at pp. 269-271.
50. 53 NJ 86, 148 A2d 521 (1968).
51. —NYS2d—(NY County, March 4, 1988).
52. —NYS2d—(NY County, February 25, 1988).
53. New York Laws 1988, chapter 475, effective January 1, 1989.

54. See New York Times (April 11, 1987) at p. 10. See Text of Kennesaw, Ga., ordinance "(a) in order to provide for the emergency management of the city, and further in order to provide for and protect the safety, security and general welfare of the city and its inhabitants, every head of household residing in the city limits is required to maintain a firearm, together with ammunition therefor. (b) Exempt from the effect of this section are those heads of households who suffer a physical or mental disability which would prohibit them from using such a firearm. Further exempt from the effect of this section are those heads of households who are paupers or who conscientiously oppose maintaining firearms as a result of belief or religious doctrine, or persons convicted of a felony."

55. Id.

56. See *New York Times* (April 21, 1987) at p. A19.

57. Fla. Const., Article 1, Section 8.

58. See 15 Fla St U L Rev 751 (1987).

59. Id. at 752.

60. Alabama: Ala. Code §13A-11-50 (1982); Alaska: Alaska Stat. §11.61.220 (1983); Arizona: Ariz. Rev. Stat. Ann. §13-3102 (1978); Arkansas: Ark. Stat. Ann. §41-3151 (1977); California: Cal. Penal Code §12025(b) (West Supp. 1987); Colorado: Colo. Rev. Stat. §18-12-105 (1986); Connecticut: Conn. Gen. Stat. Ann. §29-28 (West 1958); Delaware: Del. Code Ann., tit. 11, §1442 (1979); Georgia: Ga. Code Ann. §16-11 126 (1984); Hawaii: Haw. Rev. Stat. §134-9 (1985); Idaho: Idaho Code §18-3302 (1979); Illinois: Ill. Ann. Stat., ch. 38, para 24-1(a) (Smith-Hurd Supp. 1987-88); Indiana: Ind. Code Ann. §35-47-2-1 (Burns 1985); Iowa: Iowa Code §724.4 (1987); Kansas: Kan. Stat. Ann. §21-4201 (1981); Kentucky: Ky. Rev. Stat. Ann. §527.020 (Michie/ Bobbs-Merrill 1985); Louisiana: La. Rev. Stat. Ann. §40-1789 (West 1977); Maine: Me. Rev. Stat. Ann., tit. 25, §2001 (Supp. 1985); Maryland: Md. Ann. Code, art. 27, §36B (Supp. 1986); Massachusetts: Mass. Gen. Laws Ann., ch. 269, §10 (West. supp. 1987); Michigan: Mich. Comp. Laws Ann. §750.227 (West Supp. 1987); Minnesota: Minn. Stat. Ann. §624.714 (West 1987); Mississippi: Miss. Code Ann. §97-37-1 (1972); Missouri: Mo. Ann. Stat. §571-030 (Vernon Supp. 1987); Montana: Mont. Code Ann. §45-8-316 (1985); Nebraska: Neb. Rev. Stat. §28-1202 (1985); Nevada: 1985 Nev. Stat. 592; New Hampshire: N.H. Rev. Stat. Ann. §159-4 (1977); New Jersey: N.J. Stat. Ann. § 2C:39-8 (West 1982); New Mexico: N.M. Stat. Ann. §30-7-2 (Supp. 1987); New York: N.Y.Penal Law §265.01 (1) (McKinney Supp. 1987); North Carolina: N.C. Gen. Stat. §14-269 (1986); North Dakota: N.D. Cent. Code §62.1-04-02 (1985); Ohio: Ohio Rev. Code Ann. §2923.12 (Anderson 1987); Oklahoma: Okla. Stat. Ann., tit. 21, §1272 (West Supp. 1987); Oregon: Or. Rev. Stat. §166.240-250 (Supp. 1987); Pennsylvania: Pa. Cons. Stat. Ann., tit. 18 §6106 (a) (Purdon 1982); Rhode Island: R.I. Gen. Laws §11-47-8 (1981); South

Carolina: S.C. Code Ann. §16-23-20 (Law. Co-op 1985); South Dakota: S.D. Codified Laws Ann. §22-14-9 (Supp. 1987); Tennessee: Tenn. Code Ann. §39-6-1701 (1982); Texas: Tex. Penal Code Ann. §46.02 (Vernon 1982); Utah: Utah Code Ann. §76-10-504 (Supp. 1987); Vermont: Vt. Stat. Ann., tit. 13, §4003 (1975); Virginia: Va. Code Ann. §18.2-308 (Supp. 1987); Washington: Wash. Rev. Code Ann. §9.41.050 (Supp. 1986-87); West Virginia: W.Va. Code §61-7-1 (1984); Wisconsin: Wis. Stat. Ann. §941.23 (West 1957); Wyoming: Wyo. Stat. §6-8-104 (1983).

61. Vt. New York Times Stat. Ann., tit. 13, section 4003 (1975).

62. See (November 13, 1988) at p. 30. The New York Times (April 3, 1989) at A10 reported that the Maryland board set up to decide what handguns may be sold in Maryland has found that it is not all that easy to define just what guns to control. (Note that the Maryland law does permit the sale of guns deemed suitable for law enforcement, for self-defense, and for sporting purposes). In general, the Maryland statute is intended to ban handguns that can be easily concealed and are poorly made of cheap, light materials. But the law does require gun purchasers to fill out forms stating, inter alia, that they have no criminal record, are not mentally impaired, and have no drug nor alcohol dependency.

California became the first state on March 13, 1989 to ban assault rifles and to prohibit the sale, possession or manufacturer of the military-style, semiautomatic guns. See New York Times (March 14, 1989) at 1 and D28. Semiautomatic weapons are defined as guns that require no manual action except a separate trigger pull to fire each bullet as distinct from machine guns which fire a rapid stream of bullets with a single trigger pull.

In sharp contrast to the foregoing, the legislature of the State of Nebraska in November 1988 amended the Nebraska Constitution guaranteeing the right to bear arms "for all persons." In part, the 1988 amendment decreed that there are "certain inherent and inalienable rights", among them life, liberty, and the right to bear arms." See New York Times (April 2, 1989) at 20.

63. See Tom Wicker, "NRA on the Ropes," New York Times (December 9, 1988) at p. A35:

> These blows to the N.R.A. in the 1988 elections were balanced, if at all, only by a Nebraska vote to amend the state constitution to guarantee the right to bear arms. Mr. Bush's election also may be a boost for the N.R.A., since he has opposed the waiting period and other gun control legislation.
>
> None of this necessarily means that the N.R.A. will not remain a powerful opponent of legislation and candidates that appear to threaten the millions of non-criminal Americans who legitimately own and want to keep guns. In all but a few states, they form a powerful voting bloc easily aroused against anything they think would deprive them of, or restrict their ability to possess, weapons they regard as theirs by right.
>
> The 1988 election returns suggest however, that such gun owners may be making sharper distinctions between real threats to their perceived interests, and such reasonable,

law-enhancing steps as the seven-day waiting period (already in effect in 22 states) and Maryland's ban on cheap concealable handguns.

If that's so, the N.R.A. will have to rethink its traditional cry-wolf tactics. It will no longer be so easy to persuade voters that restraints aimed only at criminals are threats to all gun owners, to the machismo of American males, even to the Constitution itself.

64. See Patterson v. State, 170 So2d 635 (Miss., 1965).
65. See City of Salina v. Blaksley, 83 P 619 (Kan., 1905).
66. See Hill v. State, 53 Ga. 473 (1874).
67. See 82 Mich L Rev 204 (Nov. 1983) at p. 207.
68. See 18 USC 922(g), (h) (1982); also note Section 12021 of Cal. Penal Code (1983).
69. See 38 U of Chi L Rev 185 (1970) at p. 205.
70. Id. at p. 206.
71. 396 US 346 (1969).
72. See Mass. Ann. Laws, Ch. 140, Section 122B (1969).
73. Infra note 69 at p. 209.
74. See Photos v. City of Toledo, 250 NE2d 916 (Ohio, 1969).
75. Infra note 67 at p. 265.
76. See United States v. Huffman, 518 F2d 80 (4th Cir., 1975), cert den 423 US 864 (1975).
77. See United States v. Ruisi, 460 F2d 153 (2nd Cir., 1972), cert den 409 US 914 (1972).
78. At pp. 42 et seq.
79. Id. at p. 43.
80. Id.
81. See 11 J of Police Sc & Admin 275 (September 1983).
82. Id. at p. 280.

7

Civil Liability for Manufacturers, Distributors, and Dealers of Firearms and Guns

7.1 INTRODUCTION

Firearms and guns are undeniably the central element in deaths and injuries that hundreds of thousands of crime victims suffer each year throughout the civilized world. It is submitted that courts have a responsibility, unfettered by constitutions and statutes, to provide a forum for these victims under various civil courses of action. Suits by victims may enhance effective gun control, which otherwise might encounter difficulty through the legislative process.[1] Indeed, courts may provide a more efficient vehicle than legislatures for dealing with gun control because judges and juries are generally free from the conflicting political pressures of the pro-gun and gun control lobbies.[2] Imposing civil liability upon manufacturers, distributors, and dealers of firearms and guns might limit the lawful and unlawful opportunity to purchase them. It has been estimated, for example, that every minute and half a handgun is used unlawfully to kill or injure some person.[3] Criminals are generally judgment-proof, and despite the fact that two thirds of the states and the District of Columbia have victim compensation laws, adequate compensation for victims is simply not possible.[4]

Civil liability may be predicated upon statutory violations,[5] upon negligent entrustment,[6] upon products liability and defective products,[7] upon strict liability for abnormally dangerous activities,[8] and even upon aiding and abetting criminal behavior.[9] However, according to ‘‘Handgun Manufacturers' Tort Liability to Victims of Criminal Shootings: A Summary of Recent Developments in the Push for a Judicial Ban of the 'Saturday Night Special' " all these "theories" have been tested and rejected.[10] The "ultrahazardous activity" theory was largely rejected because "judicial interpretation has generally limited this cause of action to activities related to land use."[11] Theories of products liability have also been rejected on the basis that handguns which are designed to propel bullets with lethal force are not legally "defective" unless there is something physically wrong with the handguns. Perhaps the resolution of this dilemma lies in a recognition that the conduct of the gun manufacturer is more important than the physical characteristics of the product. A product manufacturer acts negligently when marketing the lethal product to a person or persons who are not reasonable and who are foreseeably within the zone of deliberate users of the weapon with intent to kill or injure other persons. Dean Prosser described a tort as "conduct which is twisted or crooked, not straight," and this delineation is very much in point.[12]

7.2 STATUTORY VIOLATIONS

The Federal Gun Control Act of 1968 as amended established broad outlines for the manufacture and sale of firearms including such restrictions as required registration of all manufacturers, distributors, and dealers; prohibition on interstate sale of handguns; bans on importation of nonsporting handguns; prohibition of the sale of firearms to certain classes; and penalties for unlawful carrying or use of a handgun during the commission of a felony, for example.[13] Does the violation of the federal statute by manufacturers, distributors, and dealers subject them only to criminal penalties or also to civil liability? A corollary question is whether compliance with the federal statute by manufacturers, distributors, and dealers precludes victims of firearms and guns from suing under any theory of liability.

It would appear that violation of statute does subject the violator to suit by the victim who has suffered death, injury, or other damage or loss.[14] The U.S. Supreme Court in the 1975 case of Cort v. Ash held that a federal statute can give rise to a private cause of action for civil liability where (1) the statute creates a federal right on behalf of the plaintiff, (2) the evidence shows legislative intent to grant the private cause of action, (3) the private cause of action is consistent with the legislative purpose and (4) the private cause of action is not in an area traditionally governed by state law.[15] However, in Decker v. Gibson Products Company a federal district court in Georgia dismissed the complaint against the firearms dealer who had knowingly sold a handgun to an ex-convict in violation of the federal Gun Control Act of 1968; the ex-convict used the gun to kill his wife, and their children sought to predicate a cause of action against the dealer upon the statutory violation by their father.[16] The court held that neither the legislative history nor policy reasons supported a private right of action for statutory violation because Congress intended only to protect the general public through administrative enforcement of the act. Furthermore, according to the Georgia federal district court, a private cause of action would not keep firearms away from illegitimate purchasers, which was the statutory purpose behind the act. However, in theory, federal statutes do give rise to a private right of action as under 42 USC 1983 against one who acted under state law, in addition to an action pursuant to the implied right-of-action doctrine. The U.S. Supreme Court, beginning with the 1980 decision in Maine v. Thibouto,[17] followed by the 1987 decision in Wright v. Roanoke Redevelopment Housing Authority,[18] has applauded enforcement of federal statutes under 42 USC 1983, subject to two prerequisies: (1) Congress did not intend that the specific statute constituted only a declaration of policy and the specific statute was not the source of judicially enforceable rights, and (2) the federal statutory scheme does not contain specific enforcement remedies that Congress intended would be the exclusive modes of enforcement. The crux of the implied right-of-action doctrine is the intent of Congress as interpreted by the highest court in Cort v. Ash.[19] However, in 1984 in Dailey Income Fund v. Fox,[20] the highest court expanded on the intent of Congress regarding private rights of action that may be discerned by "examining a number of factors, including the legislative history and purposes of the statute, the identity of the claims for whose particular benefit the statute was passed, the existence of express statutory remedies adequate to serve the legislative purpose, and the traditional role of the States in affording the relief claimed."[21]

Imposing civil liability upon manufacturers, distributors, and dealers of firearms and guns for violation of statute would undoubtedly increase their operating costs, and they would simply pass the increased costs on to purchasers. The high costs of arms might militate against increased sales and serve as a partial deterrent to the use of firearms and guns.

7.3 NEGLIGENT ENTRUSTMENT

The cause of action in negligent entrustment originates in the permission granted for another to use the instrumentality under circumstances that evince, or should evince, an unreasonable risk of harm to other persons. Manufacturers, distributors, and dealers in firearms and guns fall into this category or delineation without question, as do indulgent parents who entrust to their speed-demon, teenage children the use of their automobiles, for example. The critical factor that determines whether an entrustment is negligent is the reasonable foreseeability of future harm to other persons resulting from entrustment of the firearm or gun to one whose habits and background bespeak untrustworthiness to control it. In Moning v. Alfono the plaintiff was injured when another child fired a slingshot and struck plaintiff in the eye.[22] The Michigan Supreme Court ruled that the slingshot manufacturer was negligent for having sold the product to children, the negligent entrustment of a dangerous weapon to a person or persons who are likely to misuse the product. A ''BB'' gun fired by a three-year-old child was deemed in Mason v. Gianotti to be a dangerous weapon negligently entrusted to a person who could use it to injure another person.[23]

Section 390 of Restatement (Second) of Torts declares that ''one who supplies directly or through a third person a chattel for the use of another, whom the supplier knows or has reason to know to be likely because of his youth, experience, or otherwise, to use it in a manner involving unreasonable risk of physical harm to himself and others whom the supplier should expect to share in or be endangered by its use, is subject to liability for physical harm resulting to them.'' Indeed, manufacturers, distributors, and dealers of firearms and guns can and should readily be required to identify potential misusers of their products. There is nothing insurmountable about ''screening'' duties being imposed upon these defendants who profitably market firearms and guns. Additional costs will undoubtedly be passed on to the purchaser, and hopefully the higher costs of firearms will deter their widespread and indiscriminate use. Negligent entrustment upholds the principle that defendants owe a duty to victims to protect them from unreasonable and foreseeable risks of harm. A safe marketing scheme to protect citizens from the risks created by negligent and reckless distribution and sale of firearms and guns is a reasonable principle upon which to predicate civil liability in favor of victims. Section 448 of Restatement (Second) of Torts further delineates the negligent entrustment theory: the defendant "at the time of his negligent conduct realized or should have realized the likelihood that a third person might avail himself of the opportunity to commit such a tort or crime."[24]

It has been suggested that if every person licensed to carry and use a firearm was required by law to carry liability insurance, the victims would then be protected, and the insurance requisite would shift the costs of violence from guns from the victim to those who own or who profit from the manufacture and sale of firearms and guns.[25] In Vic Potamkin Chevrolet, Inc. v. Horne[26] the Florida appellate court held that an automobile dealer who sold a car to someone he had seen to be a dangerous driver was held liable on the "negligent entrustment" theory to a third person later injured by the buyer. It seems that the automobile salesman learned that the buyer was a poor driver when, on a test drive, he had to wrestle the steering wheel from the driver to stop her from hitting a bus. According to the court, "One who supplies directly or through a third party a chattel for the use of another whom the supplier knows or has reason to know to be likely because of his youth, inexperience, or otherwise, to use it in a manner involving unreasonable risk of physical harm to himself and others whom the supplier should expect to share in or be endangered by its use, is subject to liability for physical harm resulting to them."

Negligent entrustment does not arise from the mere existence of a parental relationship, making the parent or parents liable for the torts of their children.[27] Indeed, a child may be responsible for his or her own torts.[28] But it is settled that a parent owes a duty to third parties to shield them from an infant's improvident use of a dangerous instrument when the parent is or should be aware of the peril and when the parent is capable of controlling the use of the dangerous instrument.[29] Gun and firearm manufacturers, distributors, and others in the chain of marketing and selling firearms and guns also have a duty to shield third parties from the improvident use of the dangerous instrumentality.

In West v. Mache of Cochran, Inc.[30] the Georgia appellate cout in 1988 held that a gun shop was negligent per se in violation of the Federal Gun Control Act[31] when it illegally sold a rifle to a former mental patient who subsequently shot and killed the victim. The plaintiff-victim demonstrated that he was a statutory beneficiary, i.e., within the group or class that the legislature was seeking to protect, that he or his decedent had suffered the type of harm the legislature was seeking to minimize or eliminate, and that the defendant's breach of the statute was a "but-for" cause or a substantial factor in bringing about the plaintiff's injury or death.[32] The defendant retailer had unlawfully sold the firearm and ammunition to the former mental patient, and therefore the defendant retailer was negligent per se and accountable for the subsequent killing of the plaintiff's wife. The court cited with approval K-Mart Enterprises of Florida v. Keller,[33] where the retailer illegally sold the firearm to the buyer [who was subject to felony information and also the unlawful user of marijuana], who entrusted the gun to his brother who then shot a police officer; Franco v. Bunyard,[34] where the retail store illegally sold the pistol to an escaped convict who thereafter killed or wounded three men whom he took as hostages; and Howard Bros. of Phoenix City, Inc. v. Penley,[35] where the retailer was liable for the sale of the handgun to a minor, mental cripple, and one high on drugs and alcohol, who later shot the plaintiff. The Federal Gun Control Act[36] specifically makes it unlawful for any licensed dealer to sell a firearm to any person who has previously been committed to a mental institution. The Georgia appellate court here concluded:

> The defendants' conduct condemns them whichever way their argument goes. If we assume that by a reasonably careful questioning and observation by a mature, experienced dealer in firearms [assailant's] condition would have been suspected, then the defendants are clearly liable. If we say that [assailant] could have masked his condition so that no layman could ever know anything about his condition, the defendants were likewise negligent. That loaded [rifles] are especially dangerous and life-threatening when possessed by mentally disturbed people is a matter of common knowledge and firearms' dealers should be especially cognizant of this. Any such dealer should have in effect in his business some safeguard to see that a loaded [gun] is not placed in the hands of an unknown person, who may very well be mentally disturbed, unless or until his background can be thoroughly investigated.

7.4 PRODUCTS LIABILITY AND THE DEFECTIVE FIREARM OR GUN

The volatile field of products liability for defective products has unfortunately not been attractive or receptive to the courts as a basis for civil liability against the manufacturer, distributor, or dealer of firearms and guns. The difficulty stems from the fact that proof of a "defect" in the product cannot readily be shown as illustrated by Patterson v.

Rohm Gesellschaft.[37] Here a store clerk was shot to death during a robbery, and his mother sued the manufacturer of the revolver used in the robbery on the basis of a defect in manufacture of the gun. But the court found no evidence of malfunction, for the revolver had done precisely what it was warranted to do, that is, to fire a bullet with deadly force. The court also rejected the notion that the product was defective because it was too easily obtained by persons who misuse it: "In order to prove causation (cause in fact) the plaintiff (mother of the deceased) would have to show that his assailant would not have acquired a handgun had the manufacturer used a non-defective system of distribution. If the assailant would have been able to purchase a handgun despite a better system of distribution, the plaintiff could not recover." The federal district court in Texas concluded that the "unconventional theories" advanced by the plaintiff here were "totally without merit, a misuse of product liability laws." "It makes no sense to characterize any product as 'defective'—even a handgun—if it performs as intended and causes injury only because it is intentionally misused. Similarly, the claim that handgun manufacturers should be responsible for keeping their products out of the hands of criminals—an admittedly impossible task—is an unsupported, tortured extension of product liability principles."

Indeed, the gravaman of a products liability suit against the manufacturer, distributor, or dealer of firearms and guns is the claim that firearms and guns should not be on the market. But where the plaintiff alleges that a particular type of firearm or gun is defective (as opposed to a claim that all firearms and guns are defective), there is a likelihood of success, as shown in Kelley v. R.G. Industries, Inc.[38] Here the Maryland court distinguished between the cheaper handguns like the "Saturday Night Special" and the more expensive handguns.[39] The cheap handguns, according to the court, are involved in crime more than other handguns, and therefore the manufacturers of the cheap guns can be held liable because they have created products that they know or should know have no legitimate social use and are in fact used by criminals to perpetrate numerous injuries and deaths. It is logical to pass the costs of the gun's use to those who can spread the risk.[40] Section 876(c) of Restatement (Second) of Torts acknowledges that the handgun manufacturer, distributor, or dealer probably "gives substantial assistance . . . (to the tortfeasor) . . . in accomplishing a tortious result, and his own conduct separately considered, constitutes a breach of duty to the third person."[41] The imposition of strict liability here was restricted to the "Saturday Night Special," despite the court's assertion that "a handgun manufacturer or marketer generally would not be liable for gunshot injuries resulting from a criminal's use of the product."[42] In essence, the "Saturday Night Special" was regarded by the Maryland court as having "little or no legitimate value" and was used primarily in criminal activity.[43] These conclusions were deemed by the court to be clearly foreseeable by the manufacturers, distributors, and dealers, and therefore the burden of the harm suffered by victims of the particular handguns could be fairly placed on the defendants instead of upon the innocent victims.

The Illinois appellate court in its 1985 decision in Riordan v. International Armament Corp. had occasion to summarize:

> A product may be found defective in design, so as to subject a manufacturer to strict liability for resulting injuries, under either of two alternative tests. First, a product may be found defective in design if the plaintiff establishes that the product failed to perform safely as an ordinary consumer would expect when used in an intended or reasonably foreseeable manner. Second, a product may alternatively be found defective in design if the plaintiff demonstrates that the product's design proximately caused his injury and the defendant fails to establish, in light of the relevant factors, that, on balance, the benefits of the challenged design outweigh the risk of danger inherent in such design.[44]

Unfortunately, the courts have not readily swung the cudgel to find defective design in firearms, except where the gun owner injures himself. In Johnson v. Colt Industries Operating Corp., the Tenth U.S. Court of Appeals in 1986 upheld a $850,000 award of actual damages and $1.25 million in punitive damages to the plaintiff who was injured when his gun accidentally discharged, allegedly due to the manufacturer's failure to equip the gun with a safety device so as to eliminate the known drop-fire design hazard.[45] The court cited the defendant's "reckless indifference to the drop-fire design hazard," a defect resulting from putting marketing and sales ahead of product safety. Similarly, in France v. Bunyard the Arkansas court observed the defective design that made the safety catch on the handgun less secure and therefore imposed liability upon the handgun seller who should have seen that the handgun purchaser, an escaped convict, would fire the weapon in connection with a robbery and injure a store clerk.[46]

The classic case against imposing liability upon the firearms manufacturer or distributor is Richman v. Charter Arms Corp.,[47] decided by the federal district court in Louisiana in 1983. The court ruled that handgun manufacturers are not strictly liable to victims of criminal shootings under Louisiana's products liability law because a product is defective only when it is unreasonably dangerous in the context of "all reasonable foreseeable uses."[48] And since products that are unreasonably dangerous when they pose greater risks than reasonable consumers expect, handguns cannot be unreasonably dangerous because their inherently dangerous nature is obvious to the reasonable consumer.[49] Thus, under Louisiana law, marketing of handguns to the general public is not unreasonable conduct, and the Louisiana legislature substantiated this conclusion by refusing to ban handguns despite the obvious risks they pose.[50] Subsequently in Martin v. Harrington & Richardson, Inc.[51] the Seventh U.S. Court of Appeals took occasion to criticize the Richman case for "blurring the distinction between strict liability for selling unreasonably dangerous products and strict liability for engaging in ultrahazardous activities." Nevertheless, the Fifth U.S. Court of Appeals in Perkins v. F.I.E. Corp.[52] indirectly affirmed the decision in the Richman case that handgun manufacturers are not liable to victims of criminal shootings. The Fifth U.S. Court of Appeals found that Louisiana case law mandated a consumer expectation standard of product defectiveness, and there was nothing wrong with the handgun in question. The court reasoned that it was common knowledge that small, concealable handguns are designed to be dangerous weapons, and therefore such handguns are not defective simply because their misuse causes human injury.[53]

It is interesting to speculate here as to propriety of applying a specific risk/utility test, as enunciated in 1978 by the California Supreme Court in Barker v. Lull Engineering Co.[54] The risk/utility test requires the plaintiff to make a prima facie showing that the allegedly defective product proximately caused the injury; then the burden shifts to the product manufacturer "to prove that the benefits of the product's design outweigh its risk of danger."[55] The Louisiana court in the Perkins case reasoned that this test could remove from the plaintiff the burden of demonstrating a functional defect in the handgun before the court could apply the risk/utility analysis, should it so be inclined.[56] Proximate causation would be extremely difficult to prove in face of the intervening criminal use of the handgun. California's highest court in the Barker case[57] had noted that the California legislature had expressly precluded California courts from applying the risk/utility test to firearms.[58]

7.5 STRICT LIABILITY AND ABNORMALLY DANGEROUS ACTIVITIES

The rationale of strict liability for abnormally dangerous activities or ultrahazardous activities lies in the assumption that certain activities, such as the manufacture and distribution and sale of firearms and guns, are so inherently dangerous that these activities create a risk of great harm to the public, notwithstanding the exercise of reasonable care by the actor. Dean Prosser had long ago observed that "defendant's enterprise, while it will be tolerated by the law, must pay its own way . . . where the defendant's activity is unusual and abnormal in the community and the danger which it threatens to others is unduly great—and particularly where the danger will be great even though the enterprise is conducted with every possible precaution. The basis of liability is the defendant's intentional behavior in exposing those in his vicinity to such a risk."[59] This ultrahazardous-activity principle emerged from the nineteenth-century English case of Rylands v. Fletcher, where the defendant had constructed a large, artificial water reservoir on his property, and the water eventually leaked and flowed underground through abandoned mine shafts onto plaintiff's adjoining property, causing severe property damange.[60] While defendant's conduct was not unreasonable, he was still totally liable for plaintiff's damages. The English rule was simply that anyone who kept anything on his land for his own purposes which "is likely to do mischief if it escape, must keep it at his peril."[61] The damages must, however, fall within the scope of risks anticipated by the actor in light of the abnormally dangerous aspects of the activity. Negligence is not relevant, and frequently proof of negligence or intent is impossible. The defendant has benefited at the risk of grave harm to the public, and therefore the risk of injury properly belongs to the errant defendant.[62]

Section 519 of Restatement (Second) of Torts provides for strict liability for abnormally dangerous activities: "(1) One who carries on an abnormally dangerous activity is subject to liability for harm to the person, land or chattels of another resulting from the activity, although he has exercised the utmost care to prevent the harm. (2) This strict liability is limited to the kind of harm, the possibility of which makes the activity abnormally dangerous." Section 520 lists six factors that a court should consider in deciding whether to label an activity as abnormally dangerous or ultrahazardous:

1. existence of a high degree of risk of some harm to the person, land, or chattels of others
2. likelihood that the harm that results from it will be great
3. inability to eliminate the risk by the exercise of reasonable care
4. extent to which the activity is not a matter of common usage
5. inappropriateness of the activity to the place where it is carried on
6. extent to which its value to the community is outweighed by its dangerous attributes

Unfortunately, Sections 519 and 520 have not proved appropriate for curbing sales of firearms and guns as illustrated by the Florida case of Trespalacios v. Valor Corp. of Florida.[63] The court refused to apply strict liability, not only because the marketing of the ''riot and combat'' shotguns was not an abnormally dangerous activity, but also because there was no allegation by the plaintiff that the shotgun was defective, nor had the marketer any duty to prevent the sale of the shotgun to dangerous people.

On the other hand, courts have traditionally applied the abnormally-dangerous-activities doctrine to such business activities as crop-dusting,[64] blasting,[65] storage of inflammable liquids,[66] and even to the disposal of hazardous waste.[67] The doctrine of abnormally dangerous activities does not seek to deter but rather to provide a method for compensating victims. Abnormally dangerous activities present unavoidable risks even after the defendant has taken reasonable precautions.[68]

An important policy consideration in delineating the abnormally dangerous activity, as indicated above, is the risk-bearing capacity of the defendant. The loss that handgun victims suffer is often catastrophic, and few victims can shift the cost of physical injury to their medical insurers. Handgun manufacturers, distributors, and dealers are in a position to compensate victims and to spread the added cost of doing business among all handgun purchasers by raising their prices. The focus, as indicated above, is not necessarily to promote a safer product but to compensate adequately the innocent victim. In short, the manufacturer, distributor, and dealer in firearms and guns pose an abnormal risk to every community, and since their activities are abnormal, should mandate the application of the strict liability doctrine.[69]

Short of strict liability is the doctrine that holds the defendant to a very high or extraordinary degree of care, as illustrated by Riley v.

McGreen.[70] The Louisiana appellate court ruled that "persons who use or handle inherently dangerous agencies, substances or instrumentalities such as explosives, electricity, *firearms*, combustibles and fireworks, which might endanger persons or property," are held to this very high or extraordinary standard of care.

7.6 AIDING AND ABETTING CRIMINAL BEHAVIOR

Section 876(b) of Restatement (Second) of Torts deals with "harm resulting to a third person from the tortious conduct of another" who "knows that the other's conduct constitutes a breach of duty and gives substantial assistance or encouragement to the other so to conduct himself." In short, aiding and abetting criminal behavior is not a far cry from aiding and abetting the tortious conduct of criminal customers. Defendants knew or should have known that firearms are being sold to people who intend to commit crimes, and yet defendants deliberately distributed the firearms so as to put them in criminals' hands. Indeed, the victim can sue and collect damages from the perpetrator as well as the aider-abettor. A comparable case in Halberstam v. Hamilton, where the U.S. Court of Appeals for the District of Columbia ruled that a spouse of a burglar who aided and abetted her husband in his burglary, even though she was not present at the burglary, was civilly liable for his crime, even including the murder committed during the burglary.[71] According to the court, "aiding-abetting includes the following elements: (1) the party whom the defendant aids must perform a wrongful act that causes an injury; (2) the defendant must be generally aware of his role as part of the overall illegal or tortious activity at the time he provides the assistance; and (3) the defendant must knowingly and substantially assist the principal violation."

7.7 ANALOGY TO LIQUOR LIABILITY

In recent years the tremendous loss of life and property due to accidents caused by liquor consumption has become a major concern of society, the legislatures, and the courts. The widespread enactment of dram shop acts, for example, has imposed strict liability upon dispensers of liquor to intoxicated persons. State courts have expanded the scope of liability for social hosts whose drunken quests cause automobile crashes[72] and for municipalities whose agencies permit drunk drivers to drive on public streets and highways.[73] The New Hampshire Supreme Court in Weldy v. Town of Kingston imposed liability on the town whose police officers stopped a car of drunk teenagers but let them go after taking their beer cans away from them; later the teenagers were fatally injured in a car accident.[74] Bartenders in Florida must spot alcoholic customers before serving them drinks[75] according to Hastings v. Sachs, Inc.[76]

Is not the distribution of firearms and guns an instance of a more anti-social behavior than unlawfully dispensing liquor to intoxicated persons? If strict liability and dram shop acts are the products of interested legislatures and responsible courts, why should not equal treatment be accorded the manufacturer, distributor, and dealer of firearms and guns whose products cause injury or death to innocent third parties or victims? The Florida case of Ritchie v. Old Republic Insurance Co. demonstrates the fatal involvement of liquor and guns, as the court expounded upon the nature and extent of the liability of a tavern for the sale of liquor to an intoxicated minor who thereupon fatally shot plaintiff's decedent.[77] The plaintiff was awarded $1.6 million because liquor and guns simply did not mix. Absolute or strict liability should be applicable to the dispensing of firearms and guns to persons with criminal intent as it is applicable to the dispensing of liquor to intoxicated persons.

NOTES

1. See 6 Hamline L Rev 351 (1983).
2. See generally 97 Harv L Rev 1912 (1984).
3. According to "Crime Victims Compensation Trust Fund," Hearing On H.R.2470 Before the Subcommittee on Select Revenue Measures of the Committee on Ways and Means, 98th Cong., 1st Sess., 8 (1983), about 350,000 victims of violent crime suffer gunshot wounds annually in the United States.
4. See 1985 Ill L Rev 967 (1985) at pp. 967-968.
5. See Section 2 of this chapter.
6. See Section 3 of this chapter.
7. See Section 4 of this chapter.
8. See Section 5 of this chapter.
9. See Section 6 of this chapter.
10. See 31 Villanova L Rev 1577 (1986).
11. Note Kelley v. R.G. Industries, 497 A2d 1143 (Md., 1985) and also Perkins v. F.I.E. Corp., 762 F2d 1250 (5th Cir., 1985).
12. Prosser on Torts (4th ed., 1971) at p. 2.
13. 18 USC 921-928 (1982).

14. Infra note 4 at p. 970.
15. 422 US 66 (1975).
16. 505 F Supp 34 (MD Ga., 1980).
17. 448 US 1 (1980).
18. 107 S Ct 766 (1987).
19. Infra note 15.
20. 464 US 523 (1984).
21. Id. at p. 536.
22. 254 NW2d 759 (Mich., 1977).
23. 388 NYS2d 322 (1976).
24. See generally Woods, ''Negligent Entrustment: Evaluation of a Frequently Overlooked Source of Additional Liability,'' 20 Ark L Rev 101 (1966).
25. See Note, ABAJ 244 (March 1982). Also, see Freedman, International Products Liability (2 vol., Kluwer, 1987) at Section 3.13.
26. So2d (Fla. App., 1986).
27. See Napiearlski v. Pickering, 106 NYS2d 28 (1951).
28. See Rozell v. Rozell, 281 N.Y. 106 (1939).
29. See Nolechek v. Gesuale, 413 NYS2d 340 (1978).
30. 370 SE2d 169 (Ga App., 1988).
31. 18 USC 922(d)(4).
32. Note Harper, James & Gray, Law of Torts (2d ed., 1986) at Sections 17.5 and 17.6.
33. 439 So2d 283 (Fla. App., 1983).
34. 547 SW2d 91 (Ark., 1977).
35. 492 So2d 965 (Miss., 1986).
36. Infra note 31.
37. 608 F Supp 1206 (ND Texas, 1985).
38. 497 A2d 1143 (Md., 1985).
39. The court described the ''Saturday Night Special'' as ''generally characterized by short barrels, light weight, easy concealability, low cost, use of cheap quality materials, poor manufacture, inaccuracy and unreliability.''
40. See generally 26 Ariz L Rev 889 (1984) and 14 Pac L J 117 (1983).
41. Note also Sections 519 and 520 of Restatement (Second) of Torts:

> (1) One who carries on an abnormally dangerous activity is subject to liability for harm to the person, land or chattels of another resulting from the activity, although he has exercised the utmost care to prevent the harm.
> (2) This strict liability is limited to the kind of harm, the possibility of which makes the activity abnormally dangerous.

> In determining whether an activity is abnormally dangerous, the following factors are to be considered:
> (a) existence of a high degree of risk of some harm to the person, land or chattels of others;

(b) likelihood that the harm that results from it will be great;
(c) inability to eliminate the risk by the exercise of reasonable care;
(d) extent to which the activity is not a matter of common usage;
(e) inappropriateness of the activity to the place where it is carried on; and
(f) extent to which its value to the community is outweighed by its dangerous attributes.

42. Id. at pp. 1150-1151.
43. Id. at pp. 1157-1158.
44. 477 NE2d (Ill. App., 1985).
45. 797 F2d 1530 (10th Cir., 1986).
46. 547 SW2d 91 (Ark., 1977), cert den 434 US 835 (1977).
47. 571 F Supp 192 (ED La., 1983).
48. Id. at 195, quoting from Le Bouef v. Goodyear Tire & Rubber Co., 623 F2d 985 (5th Cir., 1980) at p. 989.
49. "[C]ommon sense requires the Court to find that the risks involved in marketing handguns for sale to the general public are not greater than reasonable consumers expect. Every reasonable consumer that purchases a handgun doubtless knows that the product can be used as a murder weapon. This knowledge, however, in no way deters reasonable consumers from purchasing handguns. . . . [W]arnings are not likely either to alter consumer buying behavior or to reduce handgun violence. The plaintiff's reliance on the 'consumer expectation' theory is therefore misplaced." (at p. 198).
50. "[T]he Louisiana legislature has neither enacted a statute banning the sale of handguns to the general public nor adopted a joint resolution to amend the Constitution to that effect. Given the prominence of the handgun issue in public debates. . . . [t]he inference the court should draw from this is clear: the legislature does not think handgun manufacturers act unreasonably (are negligent per se) when they market their product to the general public. . . . Any other view . . . would appear to be implausible" (at p. 198).
51. 743 F2d 1200 (7th Cir., 1984).
52. 762 F2d 1250 (5th Cir., 1985).
53. See 31 Villanova L Rev 1577 (1986) at pp. 1600-1601.
54. 573 P2d 443 (Calif., 1978).
55. Infra note 52 at p. 1273.
56. Infra note 52.
57. Infra note 54.
58. Infra note 55 at pp. 1273-1274.
59. See Prosser on Torts (4th ed., 1971) at p. 494.
60. 3 H & C 774, 159 Eng Rep 737 (1865), re'd LR 1 Exch 265 (1866), aff LR 3 HL 330 (1868).
61. Id.
62. See 31 Villanova L Rev 2577 (1986) at p. 1586.
63. 486 So2d 649 (Fla., 1986).

64. See Langan v. Valicopters, Inc., 567 P2d 74 (Wash., 1977).

65. See Liber v. Flor, 415 P2d 332 (Colo., 1966).

66. See Zero Wholesale Gas Co. v. Stroud, 571 SW2d 74 (Ark., 1978).

67. See Village of Wilsonville v. SCA Services, Inc., 426 NE2d 824 (Ill. App., 1981); and also see Warren Freedman, Hazardous Waste Liability (Michie, 1987).

68. See Fontenot v. Magnolia Petroleum Co., 80 So2d 845 (La., 1955).

69. Note Martin v. Harrington and Richardson, Inc., 743 F2d 1200 (7th Cir., 1984) where the federal appellate court stated that, while the use of handguns is clearly an ultrahazardous activity under state law, the sale of nondefective handguns is not an ultrahazardous activity under state law. Note Delahanty V. Hinckley, 686 F Supp 920 (DC., 1988) to the effect that a nonresident handgun manufacturer and the local distributor of the handgun cannot be held strictly liable for the manufacturer and distribution of "Saturday Night Specials." The court in the District of Columbia opined that to impose such a standard of strict liability would exempt from liability manufacturers of toerh guns that may also have been sued for criminal activity.

70. 427 So2d 509 (La., 1983).

71. 705 F2d 472 (D.C. Cir., 1983). The court concluded:

> Tort law is not, at this juncture, sufficiently well developed or refined to provide immediate answers to all the serious questions of legal responsibility and corrective justice. It has to be worked over to produce answers to questions raised by cases such as this. Precedent, except in the securities area, is largely confined to isolated acts of adolescents in rural society. Yet the implications of tort law in this area as a supplement to the criminal justice process and possibly as a deterrent to criminal activity cannot be casually dismissed. We have seen the evolution of tort theory to meet 20th century phenomena in areas such as product liability; there is no reason to believe it cannot also be adapted to new uses in circumstances of the sort presented here. This case is obviously only a beginning probe into tort theories as they apply to newly emerging notions of economic justice for victims of crime.

72. See McGuiggan v. New England Telephone Co., 196 NE2d 141 (Mass., 1986).

73. See ABAJ (Dec. 1, 1986) at p. 37.

74. 514 A2d 1257 (N.H., July 17, 1986).

75. See Fla. Stat. Sec. 768.125 (eff May 24, 1980).

76. So2d (Pinellas County, Fla., Nov. 1, 1986).

77. So2d (Fla., 1986).

8

Where Do We Go from Here?

The previous seven chapters have delineated in great detail the terminology and meaning of the Second Amendment, the historical perspective on keeping and bearing arms, the judicial interpretation given to the Second Amendment, the limitations on the privilege to keep and bear arms, firearms and gun control legislation, both federal and state, and the concept of civil liability for manufacturers, distributors, and dealers of firearms and guns. The powerful National Rifle Association has bitterly fought to retain its status as the prime advocate of the ''right'' to keep and bear arms. The NRA has long framed the debate around other issues; it insists that gun control legislation violates gun owners' constitutional rights, that tough laws constitute an unwarranted intrusion on the gun owners' privacy, and that gun control legislation does little to stop crime.[1] Congressman Edward F. Feighan of Ohio has pointed out that ''while the killing continues, the lobby's strident rhetoric and strong political-action committee have stifled debate and stalled constructive efforts to regulate the traffic in guns. With handguns causing 20,000 fatalities and countless injuries each year, the NRA's position must be rigorously scrutinized.''[2] Congressman Feighan concludes that ''what this lobby does not say is that this supposedly unassailable (constitutional) right is solely directed to maintaining a 'well-regulated Militia'. . . . In short, statutory regulation of gun sales does not necessarily infringe upon the constitutional right to bear arms.'' On the right of privacy[3] the congressman contends that ''sound public policy must balance the gun owner's right to privacy against a potential victim's right to life.''[4] The congressman calls for a federal statute with teeth to control the sale of handguns.[5]

The U.S. Supreme Court in its 1986 decision in McLaughlin v. United States[6] stated that even an unloaded handgun was a ''dangerous weapon'' within the meaning of the federal bank robbery statute.[7] The court observed that a gun is typically and characteristically dangerous, the use for which it is made and sold is dangerous, that the law may presume that such an article is always dangerous even though the gun may be unloaded. Displaying a gun instills fear in the average citizen and creates an immediate danger that a violent response will ensure, according to the highest court. The accidental discharge of a .22 caliber revolver causing death prompted the Tenth U.S. Court of Appeals in Johnson v. Colt Industries Operating Corp. to uphold a jury award of $850,000 in compensatory damages and $1.25 million in punitive damages against the manufacturer of the defective revolver; the manufacturer had failed to equip the revolver with a safety device to eliminate the known hazard of ''drop fire,'' which occurs when the revolver is carried with a bullet in the chamber over the hammer rests.[8]

The thrust of the foregoing is simply that firearms and guns have little, if any, social utility. In Kelley v. R.G. Industries the highest Maryland court said that, if manufacturers create products that they know or should know have no legitimate social use and are in fact used by criminals to perpetrate numerous injuries and deaths, it is perfectly logical to pass the costs of the gun's use to those who can spread the risk, specifically the gun manufacturer, gun distributor, and gun dealer.[9] In substance, as stated in Section 876(c) of Restatement (Second) of Torts, the gun manufacturer ''gives substantial assistance to the other in accomplishing a tortious result, and his own conduct separately considered, constitutes a breach of duty to the third person.''

The moral aspect of a defendant's conduct, that is, the moral guilt or blame to be attached in the eyes of society to the defendant's acts, motives, and state of mind, must be taken into consideration in validating gun control legislation. The oppressor, the perpetrator of outrage, the knave, the liar, the scandal-monger, the person who does spiteful harm for its own sake, the selfish aggressor who deliberately disregards and overrides the interests of neighbors, and, yes, the gun manufacturers, distributors, and dealers, may expect to find that the courts of society, no less than the opinion of society itself, condemn such conduct or activity.[10] The twentieth century has seen the development of new fields of liability in which defendants are even held liable for well-intentioned and reasonable conduct because society considers that their enterprises should pay their way by bearing the losses they inflict upon others. Tort law is but another means of deterring the sales and uses of firearms and guns which lack social use.

Mr. Justice Lewis Powell, who retired as Associate Justice of the U.S. Supreme Court, addressed the annual meeting of the American Bar Association in Toronto in August 1988. He expressed his doubt that the Second Amendment created any right to own handguns, particularly since guns contribute to the shocking number of murders in the United States. He said that the FBI reported 20,096 murders were committed in 1987 and 20,613 murders in 1986, and that 60 percent of the murders were committed with firearms.[11] According to Justice Powell, in England and Wales there were only 662 homicides in 1986, and only 8 percent were committed with firearms: ''Private ownership of handguns is strictly controlled in other Western democracies. In Great Britain, for example, gun owners must apply for a special license and satisfy the authorities that their possession of firearms will not endanger public safety. . . . Firearms dealers are strictly regulated and subject to record-keeping requirements.'' Justice Powell observed that the American Bar Association had in 1965 (while he was its president) adopted a resolution approving appropriate regulation of the sale and ownership of handguns, but apparently to no avail. (The ABA in 1973, 1975, and 1983 adopted similar resolutions, all to no avail; in 1988 an ABA representative testified in favor of the seven-day waiting period bill before the House of Representatives, which promptly defeated the bill.)

Of more than passing interest are the conclusions set forth in Volume 49 of Law & Contemporary Problems (Winter 1986):

1. Gun control laws should be aimed at restricting gun possession among persons with prior records of violence rather than among the general public. Otherwise, loss of the deterrent effect on crime exerted by widespread civilian gun ownership could outweigh the benefit of a slight reduction in gun possession among the violence-prone.

2. Gun control restrictions should be applied equally to all types of firearms, not just to handguns or ''Saturday Night Specials.'' An inclusive approach would avoid inadvertently encouraging the substitution of deadlier weapons,

a distinct possibility not precluded by marginal differences in concealability between the gun types.

3. Beyond amending the Gun Control Act of 1968 to make evasion of state gun control laws more difficult, further legislation at the federal level is unnecessary, given the greatly varying need for gun control among the states.
4. Unless the priority criminal justice system personnel assign to enforcing gun laws changes, any additional enactments must depend primarily on voluntary compliance for their effectiveness. It is doubtful whether additional resources would be made available for enforcement of gun laws, unless the revenues were somehow specifically attached to specialized gun law enforcement agencies.
5. Gun control measures must deal with the fact that criminals obtain their guns primarily through private, quasi-legal transfers from private parties such as friends or acquaintances ''on the street,'' rather than from licensed dealers, black market enterprises, or through theft. Such transfers might be minimized by establishing civil liability for damages resulting from an illegal gun transfer to an ineligible recipient. Transfers of firearms would be channeled through dealers who would be required to examine certain legal documents (driver's license, purchase permit, owner's license) to establish that the recipient was eligible. Persons who transferred guns in any other manner would be liable for damages caused with the gun by any ineligible recipient to whom they transferred the gun.

These conclusions do not coincide entirely with this author's tenets in the following respects: Item 1 is too restrictive, for the simple reason that prior records of crime may be wholly untrustworthy and there may be more crime and violence in the ''general public.'' There is no loss of deterrence by broadening the exclusion for restricting gun possession. Item 2 is meaningful if the sense is a total ban on all firearms and guns, not merely handguns and concealable weapons. Item 3 should be amended to call for enhanced federal gun controls that can supplement state gun control laws when states call upon federal agencies for assistance. Item 4 does mandate a tax on the manufacture, distribution, and sale of firearms and guns, and that revenue could well pay for the necessary administrative costs of full-fledged enforcement of gun control laws, federal, state, and local. And Item 5 is the realistic appraisal of how guns and firearms find their ways into the hands of the criminal element in society. Civil liability in the products liability arena is but one step in the direction of holding those in the chain of manufacture, distribution, and sale of firearms and guns legally responsible for the consequent injuries and death caused by their use.

NOTES

1. See Feighan, ''A Way to Control Handguns,'' New York Times (April 15, 1987) at p. A27.
2. Id. For an update on what's new in gun manufacturing, see New York Times (April 2, 1989) at D4, headline ''reeling from a wave of anti-gun sentiment,'' ''hard times: gun makers retrench and toughen their tactics,'' ''a drive to woo women—and invigorate sales,'' and ''moving hunting rifles away from the target of a ban.''
3. See Freedman, The Right of Privacy in the Computer Age (Quorum Books, 1986).
4. Infra note 1.
5. Id.
6. 106 S Ct 1677 (1986).
7. 18 USC 2113(d) (1982).
8. 797 F2d 1530 (10th Cir., 1986).
9. 497 A2d 1143 (Md., 1985).
10. See Prosser and Keeton on Torts (1984) at p. 21.
11. See A.B.A.J. (October 1, 1988) at 30.

Bibliography

On a more general basis, see ''Gun Control and Constitutional Rights,'' Hearing Before the Subcommittee on the Constitution of the Committee of the Judiciary, U.S. Senate, 96th Cong., 2nd Sess., September 15, 1980, Serial No. 96-83, at 720-735, reproduced on the following pages:

VANCE BIBLIOGRAPHICS, PUB. ADM. SERIES, BIBLIOGRAPHY NO. 554

GUN CONTROL AND THE SECOND AMENDMENT

(By Earleen H. Cook, Business and Social Sciences Librarian, The University of Texas at Arlington, and Joseph Lee Cook, Assistant University Librarian, Mary Couts Burnett Library, Texas Christian University)

INTRODUCTION

For many years the issue of gun control in the United States has raised the emotional response of the public. Assinations, both attempted and successful, of the past seventeen years have provoked advocates both of control and non-control to speak out with the same fervor as the pro and anti-abortionists.

This survey of the literature presents a selection of publications since 1960 which, hopefully, will assist the reader in a review of both sides of a most controversial topic in the United States.

Ace, C. "Arms and the Disturbed Man," "Saturday Review, L. September 16. 1967, 12.

"Act 696: Robbing the Hunter, Hunting the Robber?" Arkansas Law Review, XXIX, Winter 1976, 570–577.

"Ahead Now on Gun Control," U.S. News and World Report, LXV, July 15 1968, 8–9.

"Aimless: Opponents of Federal Legislation to Control Firearms," Time, LXXXVIII, September 9, 1966, 25.

Alviani, Joseph D. and William R. Drake. Handgun Control. . . . Issues and Alternatives. Washington: Handgun Control Project, U.S. Conference of Mayors, 1975.
American Bar Foundation. Firearms and Legislative Regulations. Chicago: The Foundation, 1967.
American Enterprise Institute for Public Policy Research. Gun Control. Washington: The Institute, 1976.
"American Politics and the Snub-Nosed Revolver," Christian Century, LXXXIX, May 31, 1972, 623.
"Another Misfire," Time, C., August 21, 1972, 8.
Anti-Defamation League. Extremism, Violence and Guns. New York: Anti-Defamation League of B'nai B'rith, 1968.
Armbrister, T. "How Many More Must Die Before Congress Acts?" Reader's Digest, C, March 1972, 96–100.
"Armed Right," Economist, CCXVI. July 24, 1965, 341.
"Arms and the Law," Sports Illustrated, XIX, December 9, 1963, 15.
Ashbrook, J. M. "Against Comprehensive Gun Control," Current History, LXXI, July 1976, 23–25+.
Ashworth, A. J. "Liability for Carrying Offensive Weapons," Criminal Law Review, December 1976, 725–736.
"Availability of Guns: A Right or a Fright? Pro and Con Discussion," Senior Scholastic, XC, March 10, 1967, 14–15.
Bakal, C. "Failure of Federal Gun Control," Saturday Review, LIV, July 3, 1971, 12–15+.
———. "Gun Control, Now; Excerpts From Right to Bear Arms," Reader's Digest, XCIII, August 1968, 83–87.
Bakal, C. No Right to Bear Arms. New York: Paperback Library, 1968.
———. "Philadelphia Story: Do Gun Control Laws Really Work?" Saturday Review, L, April 22, 1967, 20–21+.
———. "Philadelphia Story: Do Gun Control Laws Really Work? Discussion," Saturday Review, L, May 13, 1967, 27; L, May 20, 1967, 33.
———. The Right to Bear Arms. New York: McGraw-Hill, 1966.
———. "Traffic in Guns: A Forgotten Lesson of the Assassination," Harper's, CCXXIX, December 1964, 62–68.
———. "Traffic in Guns: A Forgotten Lesson of the Assassination. Discussion," Harper's CCXXX, February 1965, 12.
Balk, A. "Firearms Theatre of the Absurd," Saturday Review, L, July 22, 1967, 28+.
Barth, A. "We Need a Firearms-Control Law, Now!" Reader's Digest, XC, January 1967, 17–18+.
Batman, T. "Case for Registering Guns," Saturday Review, XLVII, August 1, 1964, 18.
———. "Case for Registering Guns. Discussion," Saturday Review, XLVII, August 22, 1964, 19+.
"Battle Against the Gun; Chicago Crimes," Time, CIV, November 4, 1974, 24+.
"Battle of the Guns; Bill to Cut Mail-Order Business," Time, LXXXV, April 16, 1965, 24–25.
Beard, M. K. "Showdown with the Gun Gang at Gun Control Corral," Business and Society Review, Fall, 1977, 67–71.
———. "Showdown with the Gun Gang at Gun Control Corral. Discussion," Business and Society Review, Summer, 1978, 65–68.
Beha, James A., II. "And Nobody Can Get You Out: The Impact of a Voluntary Prison Sentence for the Illegal Carrying of a Firearm, or the Use of Firearms and on the Administration of Criminal Justice in Boston," Boston University Law Review, LVII, January 1977, 96–146; March 1977, 289–333.
Benenson, Mark K. "Controlled Look at Gun Controls," New York Law Forum, XIV, Winter, 1968, 718–748.
Bennett, J. V. "Gun and How to Control It," New York Times Magazine, September 25, 1966, 34–35+.
Bessick, Elmer A. "Gun Control Statutes and Domestic Violence," Cleveland State Law Review, XIX, September 1970, 556–567.
"Be Strong, Carry a Gun," New Republic, CXLIX, December 14, 1963, 7.
"Big New Drive for Gun Controls," U.S. News and World Report, LXXVIII, February 10, 1975, 25–27.
Block, I. "Gun Control," Society, XIV, January 1977, 10.

Block, Irvin. Gun Control: One Way to Save Lives. New York Public Affairs Committee, 1976. (Public Affairs Pamphlet, No. 536).
Bloomgarden, Henry S. The Gun: A "Biography" of the Gun That Killed John F. Kennedy. New York: Grossman Publishers, 1975.
"Boom in the Suburbs: Philadelphia Law," Sports Illustrated, XXIII, November 1, 1965, 8.
Brill, Steven. Firearm Abuse: A Research and Policy Report. Washington: Police Foundation, 1977.
Brister, B. "What is the Real Handgun Issue?" Field and Stream, LXXVIII, March 1974, 51–53+.
Brogan, Denis W. "Murder, Incorporated or the Last, Best Hope of Earth?" Interplay, II, August/September 1968, 4–8.
Browning, Charles H. "Suicide, Firearms and Public Health," American Journal of Public Health, LXIV, April 1974, 313–317.
Bruce-Briggs, B. "Great American Gun War," Public Interest, Fall, 1976, 37–62.
Buckley, W. F., Jr. "Great American Gun War," National Review, XXIX, February 18, 1977, 223.
———. "Stampede: Senator Dodd's Firearms Bill," National Review, XVIII, August 23, 1966, 821.
———. "Triggering a New Worry: Thefts of Firearms Skyrocketing in the U.S." Wall Street Journal, CLXXXIII, January 3, 1974, 26.
"Bullet-Proof Politics?" Economist, CCXXIX, December 21, 1968, 31.
Burnett, B. "Antiquated Gun Laws," Contemporary Review, CCV, November 1964, 593–594+.
Burns, J. M. "Child's View of Gun-Control," Police Chief, XLII, December 1975, 10.
"Businessmen Recoil; Urge Tougher Gun Controls," Business Week, June 8, 1968, 42+.
Canavan, F. "Gentle Thoughts on Murder," America, CX, April 11, 1964, 503.
Caplan, David I. "Restoring the Balance: The Second Amendment Revisited," Fordham Urban Law Journal, V, Fall, 1976, 31–53.
Carmichel, J. and M. J. Harrington, eds. "Great Firearms Debate," Outdoor Life, CLVII, January 1976, 65–65+.
Casady, Margie. "Attorney General's Gun Control Plan—Good as Far as It Goes," Psychology Today, IX, July, 1975, 42.
Christopher, M. "Guns, Congress and the Networks," Nation, CCVII, August 19, 1968, 115–116.
Compton, Lynn D. "California Peace Officers, D.A.'s Adopt Gun Control Legislative Policy," American Criminal Law Quarterly, Summer 1969, 253.
Conley, C. "Federal Gun Control Act of 1968," Field and Stream, LXXVI, November 1971, 4.
"Constitutional Limitations on Federal Firearms Control," Washburn Law Journal, VIII, Winter 1969, 238+.
"Constitutional Limitations on Firearms Regulations," Duke Law Journal August 1969, 773+.
"Controls and Responsibility," Christianity Today, XVII, March 16, 1973, 27–28.
"Controversy Over Proposed Federal Handgun Legislation," Congressional Digest, LIV, December 1975, 289–314.
"Cooling It," New Republic, CLX, May 30, 1970, 11.
Cooney, Ronald F. "A Freedom Under Fire," Freeman, XXV, November 1975, 673–676.
Costa, S. "Transport Your Arms Legally," Field and Stream, LXXVIII, March 1974, 236+.
Cottin, Jonathan. "Washington Pressures—National Rifle Association," CPR National Journal, April 1970, 946–952.
Courtney, Phoebe. Gun Control Means People Control. Littletown, Colo.: Independent American Newspaper, 1974.
"Crackdown on Criminals Using Guns?" U.S. News and World Report, LXV, September 30, 1968, 7.
Crane, R. C. "Can We Stop the Anti-Gun Cranks?" Field and Stream, LXIV, Januuary 1960, 25+.
"Crime Bill Passes, What It Calls For," U.S. News and World Report, LXIV, June 17, 1968, 6.
Cupps, S. "Evading Gun Control: Public Hearings on Proposed Rules," New Republic, CLX, May 3, 1969, 16–18.

Darst, S. "Violent Majority; Attempt to Pass Gun Control Bill in St. Louis," Harper's CCLII, April 1976, 28+.
Davidson, Bill R. To Keep and Bear Arms. 2d ed. Boulder, Colo.: Sycamore Island, 1979.
"Death in the Post," Economist, CCVI, February 9, 1963, 506–507.
Deedy, J. "News and Views: Exaltation of Guns and the Shooting Sports," Commonweal, LXXXVIII, May 3, 1968, 194.
———. "News and Views: Exaltation of Guns and the Shooting Sports. Discussion," Commonweal, LXXXVIII, May 24, 1968, 283; June 7, 1968, 347+.
———. "News and Views: Gun Control Act of 1968 Amendments," Commonweal, LXXXIX, Februray 28, 1969, 664.
Defensor, H. Charles. Gun Registration Now—Confiscation Later? New York: Vantage Press, 1970.
"Defying the Gun Lobby," Nation, CCXL, September 28, 1970, 262.
Deiker, T. E. "My Neighbor is Going to Kill Me," Newsweek, LXXXIII, February 11, 1974, 12–13.
Deutsch, Stuart Jay and Francis B. Alt. "The Effect of Massachusetts' Gun Control Law on Gun-related Crimes in the City of Boston," Evaluation Quarterly, I, November 1977, 543–568.
Diamond, J. E. "Do Gun-control Laws Miss the Mark?" McCall's, CVII, November 1979, 67.
Diener, Edward and Kenneth W. Kerber. "Personality Characteristics of American Gun Owners," Journal of Social Psychology, CVII, April 1979, 227–238.
"Disarmament at Home," Nation, CCXI, December 21, 1970, 643–644.
Dodd, T. J. "Let's Limit the Sale of Guns," McCalls, XCIII, November 1965, 166+.
Dodd, T. J. "Mail-order Guns: A Senator Battles to Stem the Deadly Tide," Ladies Home Journal, LXXXII, March 1965, 74–75+.
Dolan, Edward F., Jr. Gun Control: A Decision for Americans. New York: Watts, 1978.
"Domestic Disarmament," Nation, CCXVIII, February 23, 1974, 227–228.
Drew, E. B. "Gun Law That Didn't Go Off: The Dodd Bill," The Reporter, XXXI, October 8, 1964, 33–35.
———. "Gun Laws That Didn't Go Off: The Dodd Bill. Discussion," The Reporter, XXXI, November 5, 1964, 6+.
Drinan, Robert F. "Gun Control: The Good Outweighs the Evil," Civil Liberties Review, III, August/September 1976, 44–59.
"Drop That Gun!" Commonweal, LXXXVIII, June 28, 1968, 428–429.
Du Bois, D. "What Do You Know About Gun Laws? Questions and Answers," Outdoor Life, CXXXV, April 1964, 12–14.
Edwards, George. "Commentary: Murder and Gun Control," Wayne Law Review, XVIII, July–August, 1972, 1335–1342.
"Effect of Federal Firearms Control on Civil Disorder," Brooklyn Law Review, XXXV, Spring, 1969, 433+.
Elguebal, Nady and M. Lee. "Alcoholism and Gun Control," Canadian Psychologist, XXII, 1977, 243–251.
Erskine, H. G. "Polls: Gun Control," Public Opinion Quarterly, XXXVI, Fall 1972, 455–469.
Evans, M. S. "Crime and Gun Control; McClure-Volkmer bill on Federal Firearms Law Reform Act," National Review, XXXI, November 9, 1979, 1434.
———. "Who Shall Write the Law?" National Review, XXX, July 7, 1978, 842.
Faber, Michael J. "Concealable Firearms and Ex-Felons," Journal of Criminal Law and Criminology, LXX, Spring, 1979, 73–76.
Feller, Peter Buck and Karl L. Gotting. "Second Amendment: A Second Look," Northwestern University Law Review, LXI, March–April, 1966, 46–70.
Fields, Sam. "Handgun Prohibition and Social Necessity," St. Louis University Law Journal, XXIII, 1979, 35–61.
"Fifty Dollars for Your Gun," Economist, CCII, September 1974, 68.
"Final Terms of Gun-Control Law," U.S. News and World Report, LXV, October 21, 1968, 11.
"Firearms—A Comparative Analysis of Proposed Federal Controls," De Paul Law Review, XV, Autumn-Winter, 1965, 164.
"Firearms and the Citizen; Pro and Con Discussion," Senior Scholastic, LXXXIII, December 13, 1963, 17.

"Firearms Being Checked by Police After They Had Been Handed in Following a Government Appeal," Illustrated London News, CCXXXIX, August 19, 1961, 297.
"Firearms Legislation," Vanderbilt Law Review, XVIII, June 1965, 1362+.
"Firearms Licensing, Registration Rejected by Senate," Congressional Quarterly Report, XXVI, September 20, 1968, 2459–2462.
"Firearms: Problems of Control," Harvard Law Review, LXXX, April 1967, 1328–1346.
"Firearms Regulations," Western Reserve Law Review, XVII, December, 1965, 569+.
"First Memorial: Passage of Gun-Control Bill in Memory of Dr. King," Nation, CCVI, April 22, 1968, 522–523.
Fisher, Joseph C. "Homicide in Detroit: The Role of Firearms," Criminology, XIV, November 1976, 387–400.
Fletcher, J. "Corresponding Duty to the Right of Bearing Arms," Florida Bar Journal XXXIX, March 1965, 167.
"For a Strong America; Article II, the Bill of Rights," Field and Stream, LXVIII, April 1964, 10–11.
Ford, C. "It Could Happen Here," Field and Stream, LXIX, April 1965, 6+.
Ford, G. R. "Gunning for Votes," Nation, CCXXIII, October 9, 1976, 324.
Frederick, K. T. Pistol Regulations; Its Principles and History. Washington, D.C.: National Rifle Association, 1972.
Friedland, M. L. "Gun Control: The Options," Criminal Law Quarterly, XVIII, December 1975, 29–71.
Furlong, W. B. and A. E. Stevenson, III, eds. "Let's Muffle the Sound of Guns," Good Housekeeping, CLXIV, January 1967, 64–65+.
Gall, Peter. "Private Crimes' Cause Cancer, Spear Efforts to Tighten Gun Laws," Wall Street Journal, CLXV, March 9, 1965, 1+.
Geekie, D. A. "New Federal Gun-Control Law Takes a Scattergun Approach," Canadian Medical Association Journal, CXIX, August 26, 1978, 262+.
Geisel, Martin S., et al. "Effectiveness of State and Local Regulation of Handguns: A Statistical Analysis," Duke Law Journal, August, 1969, 647.
Gemmil, Henry. "Domestic Disarmament: Strict Restrictions on Private Guns May Prove Inevitable," Wall Street Journal, CLXXI, July 6, 1968, 14.
Getting Serious About Handguns. Boston: Massachusetts Research Center, 1976.
"GH Poll: Should a Permit Be Required to Purchase a Gun?" Good Housekeeping, CLXVI, May 1968, 28+.
Gillis, A. "Guns of November," Mcclean's, XCI, November 20, 1978, 20.
Glassen, Harold W. "Firearms Control: A Matter of Distinction," Trial, VIII, January-February, 1972, 52+.
"Glory of Guns: Gun Control Magazines Campaign Against Legal Control of Gun Sales," Time, XC, August 25, 1967, 62–63.
"Going Armed: Report of National Commission of the Causes and Prevention of Violence," Nation, CCIX, December 8, 1969, 621.
Goldwater, B. "Why Gun-Control Laws Don't Work." Reader's Digest, CVII, December 1975, 183–184+.
Good, P. "Blam! Blam! Blam! Not Gun Nuts, But Pistol Enthusiasts," New York Times Magazine, September 17, 1972, 28–29+.
———. "Blam! Blam! Blam! Not Gun Nuts, But Pistol Enthusiasts. Discussion." New York Times Magazine, October 15, 1972, 29+.
Gottlieb, Alan B. The Gun Owner's Political Action Manual. Ottawa, Ill.: Green Hill, 1976.
Grahame, A. "Gun Owner's Shouls Switch to the Offense." Outdoor Life, CXXXII, November 1963, 10–11+.
Great Britain. Home Office. The Control of Firearms in Great Britain: A Consultative Document. London: HMSO, 1973.
Greenwood, Colin. Firearms Control: A Study of Armed Crime and Firearms Control in England and Wales. London: Routledge and Kegan Paul, 1972.
Gruening, Ernest. "Should We Have Federal Registration of Firearms? No," American Legion Magazine, LXXXV, December 1968, 16–17.
——— "Should We Have Federal Registration of Firearms? "Yes," by Charles H. Percy, American Legion Magazine, LXXXV, December 1968, 16–17.
"Gun Battle Heats Up," Business Week, June 15, 1968, 38–39.
"Gun Battle: Senator Dodd's Firearms Control Bill," Commonweal, LXXXII, May 28, 1965, 209.

"Gun Control," Congressional Quarterly Weekly Report, XXVI, June 21, 1968, 1557, 1558.
"Gun Control," New Republic, CLIX, September 21, 1968, 11-12.
"Gun Control," Senior Scholastic, CII, April 23, 1973.
"Gun Control: A Senate Vote to Crack Down on Handguns, But," U.S. News and World Report, CXXIII, August 21, 1972, 37.
"Gun Control and Public Order," Nation, June 7, 1971, 706-707.
"Gun Control Confusion: Gun Control Act of 1968," Conservationist, XXIII, April 1969, 23-36.
"Gun Control: Melodrama, Farce and Tragedy," Christian Century, LXXXV, June 26, 1968, 831-832.
"Gun Control Serial," Nation, CCXIV, June 5, 1972, 708-709.
"Gun Controls," Congressional Quarterly Weekly Report, XXVI, August 2, 1968, 2047-2049.
"Gun Controls: Aimless or on Target? Pro and Con Discussion," Senior Scholastic, XCIII, September 13, 1968, 19-20.
"Gun Controls Extended to Long Guns, Ammunition," Congressional Quarterly Weekly Report, XXVI, October 18, 1968, 2834-2836.
"Gun Controls, How They Work in Other Countries," U.S. News and World Report, LXIV, June 24, 1968, 38-39.
"Gun Controls: Indispensable or Irresponsible? Pro and Con Discussion," Senior Scholastic, XCI, December 7, 1967, 5-7.
"Gun Controls: 1973 Effort Will Renew Old Conflict," Congressional Quarterly Weekly Report, XXXI, March 10, 1973, 523-529.
"Gun Controls: Where They Stand, What's Ahead," U.S. News and World Report, LXV, July 1, 1968, 6.
"Gun Foes Hit Home," Business Week, June 22, 1968, 33.
"Gun for Christmas," Economist, CCXXIX, December 1, 1968, 31.
"Gun in Law," Economist, CCXLIII, June 3, 1972, 46.
"Gun Law," Economist, CCXIV, February 20, 1965, 791.
"Gun Law, A Step Toward Sanity," Life, LXIV, May 10, 1968, 4.
"Gun Law Enfeeblement," America, CXXI, December 6, 1969, 553.
"Gun Law in London," Economist, CCXLVI, February 24, 1973, 16.
"Gun Laws Shouldn't Be Aimed Wildly at all Sportsmen," Saturday Evening Post, CCXXXII, February 13, 1960, 10.
"Gun (or Two) In Every Home," Nation, CCVI, January 15, 1968, 69.
"Gun Registration: Will It Help?" Santa Clara Lawyer, XI, September 1971, 401.
"Gun Under Fire," Time, XCI, June 21, 1968, 14-18.
Gunderson, A. "Editors Don't Agree on Gun Control Laws," Editor and Publisher, C, October 28, 1967, 55-56.
"Gunning for Reform," Economist, CCXXVIII, July 13, 1968, 33-34.
"Gunning for the System," Economist, CCXLV, November 4, 1972, 51.
"Guns and Riots," New Republic, CLVII, August 5, 1967, 4.
"Guns and the Law," Economist, CCXX, August 6, 1966, 541-542.
"Guns: Like Buying Cigarettes," Newsweek, LXXI, June 17, 1968, 46.
"Guns of Boston: Bartley-Fox Law," Time, VCIII, August 2, 1976, 41.
"Guns of July, 1968; Shootings Indicate Need for Control," Newsweek, LXXII, July 15, 1968, 21-22.
"Guns on Capitol Hill," Nation, CCVI, June 24, 1968, 813.
"Gun-Toting Nation; Stricter Arms Licensing," Time, LXXXVIII, August 12, 1966, 15.
Handgun Laws of the U.S. Fairfield, Conn.: Barnes, 1974.
"Handgun Violence," New Republic, CLXVIII, February 17, 1973, 9.
"Handguns and Homicide," America, CXXV, September 11, 1971, 135.
Hardy, David T. "Firearm Ownership and Regulation: Tackling an Old Problem With Renewed Vigor," William and Mary Law Review, Winter, 1978, 235-290.
——— and John Stampoly. "Of Arms and the Law," Chicago-Kent Law Review, LI, Summer 1974, 62-114.
Hardy, David T. "Return Fire From a Gun Man," Business and Society Review, XXVI, Summer, 1978, 65-68.
Harrington, J. "Politics of Gun Control: With Editorial Comment," Nation, CCXVIII, January 12, 1974, 41-45.
Harris, R. "Annals of Legislation," New Yorker, XLIV, April 20, 1968, 56-58+.
———. "Reporter at Large: Work of the National Council to Control Handguns," New Yorker, LII, July 26, 1976, 53-54+.

Harvard University. Law School. Center for Criminal Justice. Gun Law Project. "And Nobody Can Get You Out": The Impact of Mandatory Prison Sentence for the Illegal Carrying of a Firearm, on the Use of Firearms and on the Administration of Criminal Justice in Boston. Cambridge: n.p., 1976.
Harvey, M. F. "They Have Gun Controls in England," National Review, XXIV. September 15, 1972, 1007+.
"Have Gun Will Kill: Mail Order Guns," Christian Century, LXXXII, June 2, 1965, 701–702.
"Hearings Start on Bill to Control Gun Sales," Congressional Quarterly Weekly Report, XXIII, June 4, 1965, 1060–1062+.
Heumann, Milton and Colin Loftin. "Mandatory Sentencing and the Abolition of Plea Bargaining: The Michigan Felony Firearm Statute," Law and Society Review, XIII, Winter 1979. 393–430.
Hiett, Robert, et al. "Study of Effectiveness of Gun Control Advertising," Journalism Quarterly, XLVI, Autumn, 1969, 592–594.
"High Noon for the Gun Lobby," Life, LXIV, June 28, 1968, 4.
Hofstadter, R. and M. Wallace, eds. "America as a Gun Culture; Excerpt From 'American Violence'," American Heritage, XXI, October 1970, 4–11+.
Holmberg, Judith V. and Michael Clancey. "People vs Handguns: The Campaign to Ban Handguns in Massachusetts," paper presented at the U.S. Conference of Mayors, 1977, Washington,
Horowitz, Edward J. "Reflections on Gun Control: Does the Problem Have Solutions or Do the Solutions Have Problems?" Los Angeles Bar Journal, LII, November 1976, 208–219.
"House Rejects Gun Registration, Licensing Proposals," Congressional Quarterly Weekly Report, XXVI, July 26, 1968, 1939–1941.
"How Guilty are Guns?" National Review, XX, July 2, 1968, 640.
Hughes, Marija Matich. Bibliography on Gun Legislation. Sacramento, Calif.: California State Library, Law Library, 1969.
Humphrey, H. "Crawfisher," Nation, CCXI, October 26, 1970, 387–388.
"Illinois Firearms Control—a High Caliber Solution Targeting the Owner," De Paul Law Review, XVII, Winter 1968, 400.
"Impact of State Constitutional Right to Bear Arms Provisions on State Gun Control Legislation," University of Chicago Law Review, XXXVIII, Fall 1970, 185–210.
Inouye, Daniel K., et al. "Problems on Gun Control—Senatorial Opinion—Symposium," Forensic Quarterly, L, 1976, 93–106.
"Interest Renewed in Firearms Control Legislation," Congressional Quarterly Weekly Report, XXIV, August 1966, 1803–1805.
"Interstate Commerce Nexus Requirement Defines for Firearms Possession by Felons," Mercer Law Review, XXIX, Spring 1978, 867–873.
"In the Works: Tighter Laws on Gun Sales," U.S. News and World Report, LV, December 9, 1963, 4.
"Is There a Right to Shoot?" Saturday Evening Post, CCXLI, July 27, 1968, 68.
Jackson, Maynard Holbrook, Jr. "Handgun Control: Constitutional and Critically Needed," North Carolina Central Law Journal, VIII, Spring 1977, 867–873.
Jacobs, R. C. and B. Spiegelberg. "Do-Nothing Gun Law," New Republic, CLIX, July 20, 1968, 19–22.
Jacobs, Robert Cooper. "Firearms Control," St. John's Law Review, XLII, January 1968, 353+.
Jacobson, Richard S. "Cure for Violence: No Law Like This One," Trial, XI, July 1975, 68–69.
Johnson, L. B. "LBJ Raps Rioters: Summary of Address, September 1967," Senior Scholastic, October 5, 1967, 40–41.
"Johnson's Gun Law, How It Would Work," U.S. News and World Report, LXV July 8, 1968, 34–35.
Kane, J. "Case Against Gun Control," Forensic Quarterly, L, 1976, 503–511.
Kane, M. "Bang! Bang! You'r Dead: Has the Right to Bear Arms Become Outmoded," Sports Illustrated, XXVIII, March 18, 1968, 70–74+.
Kates, D. B., Jr. "Against Civil Disarmament," Harper's CCLVII, September 1978, 28+.
———. "Gun Control: The Real Facts; Excerpt From 'Handgun Restrictions'," Field and Stream, LXXXIV, July 1979, 34–35+.
———. "Handgun Control: A Different View," Field and Stream, LXXXIII, May 1978, 46+.

———. "Reflections on the Relevancy of Gun Control," Criminal Law Bulletin, XIII, March/April, 1977, 119–124.
———. Restricting Handguns: The Liberal Skeptics Speak Out. Thornwood, N.Y.: Caroline House, 1979.
Kates, Don B., Jr. "Some Remarks on the Prohibition of Handguns," St. Louis University Law Journal, XXIII, 1979, 11–34.
———. "Why a Civil Libertarian Opposes Gun Control," Civil Liberties Review, III, June/July 1976, 24–32.
Kennedy, F. M. "Need for Gun Control Legislation," Current History, LXXI, July 1976, 26–28+.
———. "Notes and Comment; Firearm Regulation Bill; Summary of Address," New Yorker, XLIX, March 10, 1973, 20.
Kennett, Lee and James L. Anderson. The Gun in America: The Origins of a National Dilemma. Westport, Conn.: Greenwood, 1975. (Contributions in American History, No. 37.)
Kessler, Felix. "The 'Gun Lobby': Pro-Firearms Interests Have Gained Strength When Assailed in Past," Wall Street Journal, CLXXI, June 18, 1968, 1+.
Ketchum, Tony, et al. "Gun Control: The Grand Jury Reports," Canadian Forum, LIV, May/June 1974, 5+.
"King's Murder, Riots Spark Demands for Gun Controls," Congressional Quarterly Weekly Report, XXVI, April 12, 1968, 805–816.
Kleck, Gary. "Capital Punishment, Gun Ownership and Homicide," American Journal of Sociology, LXXXIV, January 1979, 882–910.
Know, N. "Another Look at New York City Gun Control Laws," Police Chief, XLII, July 1975, 10–11.
Kopkin, A. "Average American Boy," New Statesman, LXXII, August 12, 1966, 220–221.
Krema, Vaclav. The Identification and Registration of Firearms. Springfield, Ill.: Thomas, 1971.
Kriss, R. P. "Gun Control: A Missed Target," Saturday Review, LV, August 26, 1972, 26.
Krug, Alan S. Does Firearms Registration Work? A Statistical Analysis of New York Sate and New York City Crime Data. Riverside, Conn.: National Shooting Sports Foundation, 1968.
———. Firearms Registration: Costs vs Benefits; a Survey of State Law Enforcement Agencies on Firearms Registration. Riverside, Conn.: National Shooting Sports Foundation, 1970.
———, ed. Model Firearms Legislation, 2d ed. Riverside, Conn.: National Shooting Sports Foundation, 1970.
Kukla, R. J. "Gun-Control," Police Chief, XLII, 1975, 75.
———. Gun Control: A Written Record of Efforts to Eliminate the Private Possession of Firearms in America. Harrisburg, Pa.: Stackpole, 1973.
Laing, Jonathan R. "Urban Arms Race," Wall Street Journal, CLXXXV, March 12, 1975, 1+.
Lamkin, Bob. The Threat of Gun Control. Minneapolis: T. S. Denison, 1972.
Landauer, Jerry. "Curbing Firearms: Violent Crimes Drop in Toledo After It Gets Law Controlling Guns," Wall Street Journal, CLXXIV, October 7, 1969, 1+.
Large, Arlen J. "D.C. Crackdown: Washington's Tough Curbs on Guns," Street Journal. CLXXXVIII, December 2, 1976, 44.
———. "The Gun Lobby Works to Defeat Lawmakers Who Support Controls," Wall Street Journal, CLXXVI, September 11, 1970, 1+.
Lerner, M. "Freedom of Guns," New Statesman, LXVIII, December 25, 1964, 984–985.
Levin, John. "Right to Bear Arms: The Development of the American Experience," Chicago-Kent Law Review, LXVIII, Fall/Winter, 1971, 148–167.
Levine, Ronald B. and David B. Saxe. "Second Amendment: The Right to Bear Arms," Houston Law Review, VII, September 1969, 1–19.
"Limited Gun Law," Time, XCII, September 27, 1968, 20.
Lindsay, J. V. "Speaking Out: Too Many People Have Guns," Saturday Evening Post, CCXXXVII, February 1, 1964, 12+.
Link, Mary. "Candidates on the Issues: Gun Control," Congressional Quarterly Weekly Report, XXXIV, April 3, 1976, 791.
———. "Gun Control Dispute Focuses on Handguns," Congressional Quarterly Weekly Report, XXXIII, April 19, 1975, 795–797+.

———. "New Gun Control Bill Sent to House," Congressional Quarterly Weekly Report, XXXIV, April 17, 1976, 914–915.
"Logic of Inversion: Crime and Gun Control," Nation, CCXVI, February 19, 1973, 228–229.
Logsdon, G. "What Farmers Say About Gun Laws," Farm Journal, XCII, September, 1968, 37+.
Loving, Nancy, et al. Organizing for Handgun Control: A Citizen's Manual. Washington, D.C.: United States Conference of Mayors, 1977.
Lynch, Mitchell C. "Disarming Move: Gun-Control Backers Focus on Organizing at the Grass Roots," Wall Street Journal, CLXXXV, June 10, 1975, 1+.
———. "Political Shoot-Out: Tough Proposal to Ban Almost All Handguns Fares Uncertain Fate in Massachusetts Vote," Wall Street Journal, CLXXXVIII, October 28, 1976, 44.
McCabe, Michael K. "To Bear Or to Ban—Firearms Control and the 'Right to Bear Arms'," Missouri Bar Journal, XXVII, July 1971, 313+.
"McCarthy on Guns," New Republic, CLVIII, June 29, 1968, 10–11.
McCreedy, Kenneth R. and James L. Hague. "Of a Policy to Limit the Use of Firearms by Police Officers," Police Chief, XLII, January 1975, 48–52.
McDonald, Lawrence Patton. "Gun Control: We Must Defend the Second Amendment," American Opinion, VIII, May 1975, 9–12+.
McKay, John W. Gun Control: A Report on a County Priority. Honolulu: Law Enforcement Planning Office, Office of Human Resources, City and County of Honolulu, 1974.
Mahler, Anthony J. and Jonathan E. Fielding. "Fire Arms and Gun Control—Public Health Concerns," New England Journal of Medicine, CCXCVII, September 8, 1977, 556–558.
Manchester, W. "Let Us Turn in Our Guns: An Act of Conscience," Good Housekeeping, CLXVII, November 1968, 85+.
"Mandatory Minimums, Sentencing—The Concept, and a Controversial New Michigan Statute," Detroit College Law Review, 1976, 575–591.
Mann, E. B. "Are Polls Believable? Harris Poll on Gun Control," Field and Stream, LXXX, February 1976, 68+.
———. "Dear Ann Landers; Reply to Comments on Gun Control," Field and Stream, LXXXI, October 1976, 142–143.
———. "For the First Time: An Even Break: Television Program Entitled Gun Control: Pro and Con," Field and Stream, LXXX, September 1976, 114–115.
———. "Gun Laws: Some Work, Some Don't," Field and Stream, LXXXI, January 1977, 72–73.
———. "Mailbag Gleannings: Saturday Night Special," Field and Stream, LXXX, April 1976.
———. "More From My Morning Mail; Gun Control," Field and Stream, LXXXI, May 1976.
———. "More on Polls and Pollsters; Reliability of Polls on Gun Control," Field and Stream, LXXXI, August 1976, 98+.
———. "News and Comment," Field and Stream, LXXXI, June 1976, 76–77.
———. "News You Can Use," Field and Stream, LXXXI, July 1976, 82–83.
———. "Our Endangered Tradition: Effect of Gun Control Laws on Hunting," Field and Stream, LXXXI, December 1976, 12+.
Mann, E. B. "Record Speaks: Congressmen's Voting Records," Field and Stream, LXXXI, November 1976, 14+.
———. "Rex and Richard . . . and Jimmy; Bureau of Alcohol, Tobacco and Firearms' Plan to Set up Computerized National Registration System," Field and Stream, LXXXIII, September 1978, 14+.
———. "Right to Bear Arms," Field and Stream, LXXXI, November 1976, 83+.
———. "They Said It: Senate Voting on Gun Control Act," Field and Stream, LXXX, March 1976, 34+.
———. "What is a Saturday Night Special?" Field and Stream, LXXX, October 1975, 22+.
———. "What Was a Hunter?" Field and Stream, LXXX, May 1875, 8+.
Mann, J. L. "The Right to Bear Arms," South Carolina Law Review, XIX, 1967, 402–414.
Marty, M. E. "Uncivil Religion; Handguns," Christian Century, XCIII, June 9, 1976, 583.

Maryland. General Assembly. Firearms Safety Committee. Report From the Maryland Firearms Safety Committee to the General Assembly of Maryland. Annapolis?: n.p., 1965.
Massachusetts. Special Commission Established to Investigate the Causes and Possible Prevention of the Current Wave of Violence and Crime in the Commonwealth. Interim Report. Boston: n.p., 1967.
Meisler, S. "Get Your Gun From the Army," Nation, CXCVIII, June 8, 1964, 568–571.
Metzdorff, Howard A. "Gun Control: A Practical Approach," Police Chief, XLII, April 1975, 76–79.
Meyer, F. S. "Right of People to Bear Arms," National Review, XX, July 2, 1968, 657.
"More Good Than Bad: Gun-Control Provision in Omnibus Crime Bill," Time, XCI, June 28, 1968, 18.
"More on Gun Control Legislation," America, CXVII, September 9, 1967, 236.
Morgenthaler, Eric. "The Guns of Texas! High Rate of Homicide Tied to the Frontier Spirit," Wall Street Journal, LXXIV, November 20, 1969, 1+.
Morris, N. and G. Hawkins. "Controlling Violence: Toward a Less Lethal Environment: Excerpts from 'Honest Politician's Guide to Crime Control,'" Current, CXI, October 1969, 48–53.
Mosk, Stanley. "Gun Control Legislation: Valid and Necessary." New York Law Forum, XIV, Winter 1968, 694–717.
"Municipal Corporations—Home Rule—City Ordinance Concerning Weapons Control is Within the Scope of the Kansas Home Rule Amendment," Kansas Law Review, XXIV, Winter 1976, 421–431.
Murray, Douglas R. "Handguns, Gun Control Laws and Firearm Violence," Social Problems, XXIII, October, 1975, 81–93.
"Muzzling Handguns," Time, CV, April 28, 1975, 26.
Nanes, A. S. "Federal Control of Firearms: Is It Necessary?" Current History, LIII, July 1967, 37–42+.
National Council for a Responsible Firearms Policy. For Firearms Policies in the Public Interest. Washington, D.C.: n.p., 1968.
National Rifle Association. Office of Legislative Affairs. Legislative Information Service. Federal Firearms Laws, n.p. 1976.
"New Fight for Gun Controls: The Proposals and Prospects," U.S. News and World Report, LXXIX, November 10, 1975, 51–52.
New Jersey. General Assembly. Committee on State Government. Public Hearing on Assembly Bill No. 165 (Concerning Regulation of Sale and Purchase of Firearms). Hearing Before the Committee on State Government, March 2, 1966, Trenton, N.J.
New Jersey, Legislature. Senate. Committee on Law, Public Safety and Defense. Alexander J. Menza. Trenton, N.J., 1976.
New Jersey, Legislature. Senate. Committee on Law, Public Safety and Defense. Public Hearing on Senate 1125 and 1126 (Gun Control). Hearing Before the Senate Law, Public Safety and Defense Committee, June 23, 1976, Trenton, N.J., 1976.
"New Shot at Guns," Economist, CCXXVII, June 22, 1968, 43.
Newton, George D. and Franklin E. Zimring. Firearms and Violence in American Life; A Staff Report Submitted to the National Commission on the Causes and Prevention of Violence. Washington, D.C.: Superintendent of Documents, Government Printing Office, 1969. (NCCPV Staff Study Series, 7).
New York (City) Criminal Justice Coordinating Council. The Case for Federal Firearms Control. New York, n.p., 1973.
New York (State) Bar Association. Committee on Federal Legislation. Federal Firearms Control. Albany: n.p., 1971.
New York (State). Committee of Investigation. Report of the New York Committee of Investigation Concerning the Availability, Illegal Possession and Use of Handguns in New York State, Howard Shapiro, Chairman. New York, 1974.
New York (State). Legislature. Joint Committee on Firearms and Ammunition. Report. Albany, 1962. (New York (State) Legislature, Legislative Document, 1962, No. 29).
New York (State). Temporary State Commission of Investigation. Report Concerning Pistol Licensing Laws and Procedures in New York State. New York, 1964.

New York. University. State Library. Legislative Research Service. Firearms Control Pro and Con; a Revised, Selected, Annotated Bibliography, 1976.
"90 Million Firearms, and Rising Rapidly; Excerpts from Statement by the National Commission on the Causes and Prevention of Violence," U.S. News and World Report, LXVII, July 28, 1969, 40–41.
"90 Million Guns," New Republic, CLXVI, June 3, 1972. 6.
"No Action Taken to Regulate Firearms Shipments," Congressional Quarterly Weekly Record. XXIII, February 5, 1965, 205–207+.
"No Chance for Quick Relief," Time. CVI, October 6, 1975, 16+.
"No Sale to SMFRSH: Refusal to Sell Gyrojet Rocket Handgun," Time, LXXXVII, April 22, 1966, 23.
"Noncombatant's Guide to the Gun Control Fight," Changing Times, XXXIII, August 1979, 33–36.
"Notes and Comment," New Yorker, XLVIII, August 5, 1972, 19; August 19, 1972, 19.
"Notes and Comment," New Yorker, LII, April 5, 1976, 27–28.
"Notes and Comment: Hart Bill Bunning Private Ownership of Handguns," New Yorker, XLVII, November 27, 1971, 40–41.
"Now Will They Listen?" America. CXVIII, June 15, 1968, 763.
Oberbeck, S. "Gun in Your Home," Good Housekeeping, CLXXVIII, March 1974, 92–93+.
———. "Safer With A Gun?" Don't Believe It!" Reader's Digest, CVI, February 1975, 136–139.
———. "Safer With A Gun?" Don't Believe It! Reply," By E. B. Mann, Field and Stream, LXXX, October 1975, 116–118+.
Oberer, Walter E. "Deadly Weapon Doctrine—Common Law Origin," Harvard Law Review. LXXV, June 1962, 1565–1576.
O'Connor, J. "Keeping Up With the Gun Control Act of 1968," Outdoor Life, CXLIV, September 1969, 68–69+.
O'Connor, J. F. and A. Lizotte. "Southern Subculture of Violence Thesis and Patterns of Gun Ownership," Social Problems, XXV, April 1978, 420–429.
Oglesby, A. "Fallacy of Gun Laws in England," Field and Stream, LXXX, March 1976, 70+.
Olds, Nicholas V. "Second Amendment and the Right to Keep and Bear Arms," Michigan State Bar Journal, XLVI, October 1967, 15–26.
"100 Million Guns in the U.S. Today," U.S. News and World Report, LXIV, June 17, 1968, 28.
"One Lesson of the Tragedy," America, CXVIII, June 22, 1968, 787.
Oster, P. R. "How One State's Gun-Control Law is Working; Massachusetts," U.S. News and World Report, LXXXI, August 30, 1976, 35.
"Outdoor Life and the Death of a President," Outdoor Life, CXL, October 1967, 32–33.
"Overkill; Judiciary Committee Votes to Postpone Further Consideration of all Gun Legislation," Newsweek, July 8, 1968, 18.
Page, W. "Black Power Smoke; Replices Not Affected by Gun Control Act of 1968, Field and Stream, LXXIV, December 1969, 64–66+.
———. "New Gun Law Does Affect Sportsmen: Gun Control Act of 1968," Field and Streams, LXXIII, February 1969, 126–128+.
———. "New Minority; Owners of Firearms," Field and Stream, LXXVI, April 1972, 62–63+.
———. "Shooter's Santa," Field and Streams, LXXII, December 1967, 70–72.
Pazen, D. Wisconsin's Laws Relating to Firearms. Madison: Wisconsin Legislative Reference Bureau, 1971.
Petzal, D. F., ed. "Editor: Bill of Rights; Right to Keep nad Bear Arms," Field and Stream, LXXXIII, March 1979, 4.
———. "Editorial: Handguns and Firearms Legislation," Field and Stream, LXXIX, October 1974, 4.
"Philadelphia Firearms Ordinance—A Case of Comprehensive Oversight," University of Pennsylvania Law Review, LXIV, February 1966, 550–560.
Phillips, Llad, et al. "Handguns and Homicide: Minimizing Losses and the Costs of Control," Journal of Legal Studies, V, June 1976, 463–478.
Pierce, Glenn L. and William J. Bowers. The Impact of the Bartley-Fox Gun Law on Crime in Massachusetts. Boston: Center for Applied Social Research, 1979.
"Pistol Prescription," Christianity Today, XVII, March 2, 1973.

"Plea for Gun Control," Ebony, XXII, January 1967, 100–101.
Police Foundation. Police Use of Deadly Force, by Catherine H. Milton, et al. Washington: The Foundation, 1977.
"Police Use of Firearms in West Virginia—An Empirical Study," West Virginia Law Review, LXXV, December 1972, 6+.
"Politics of Problems," Nation, CCXII, June 21, 1971, 770.
"Pressure Mounts on Congress for Tough Gun Controls," Congressional Quarterly Weekly Review, XXVI, June 14, 1968, 1464–1465.
"Presumptive Possession of Weapons: New York's Controversial Statute," Buffalo Law Review, Summer, 1978, 493–509.
"The Question of Enacting Proposed Federal 'Gun Control' Legislation: Pro and Con," Congressional Digest, XLV, December 1966, 289–314.
"Question of Guns," Newsweek, LXXI, June 24, 1968, 81–85.
Reed, John Shelton. "To Live—and Die—in Dixie: A Contribution to the Study of Southern Violence," Political Science Quarterly, LXXXVI, September 1971, 429–443.
Rickenbacker, W.F. "Right to Bear Arms," National Review, XXVII, August 15, 1975, 886.
Ridgeway, J. "Don't Wait, Buy a Gun Now!" New Republic, CL, June 6, 1964, 9–10.
———. "Fun With Guns in the United States Senate," New Republic, CL, February 22, 1964, 6–7.
———. "Kind of Gun Control We Need," New Republic, CLVIII, June 22, 1968, 10–11.
"Rifles: Target for Control?" Newsweek, LXIV, December 28, 1964, 21–23.
Rigert, J. "Playing American Roulette," Commonwealth, XC, April 4, 1969, 72–75.
"Right to Bear Arms," Newsweek, LXII, December 9, 1963, 70–71.
"Right to Bear Arms," South Carolina Law Review, XIX, 1967, 402+.
"Right to Bear Arms, a Study in Judicial Misinterpretation," William and Mary Law Review, II, 1960, 381+.
"Right to Bear Arms in Pennsylvania: The Regulation of Possession," Duquesne Law Review, XI, Summer, 1973, 557+.
"Right to Keep and Bear Arms," Drake Law Review, XXVI, 1976/1977, 423–444.
"Right to Keep and Bear Arms: A Necessary Constitutional Guarantee or an Outmoded Provision of the iBll of Rights?" Albany Law Review, XXXI, January 1967, 74+.
Riley, Robert J. "Shooting to Kill the Handgun: Time to Martyr Another American 'Hero'." Journal of Urban Law, LI, February, 1974, 491–524.
———. "Shooting to Kill the Handgun: Time to Martyr Another American 'Hero'. A Reply to Advocates of Gun Control," by Jonathan A. Weiss, Journal of Urban Law, LI, February 1974, 491–524.
"Rising Demands for Gun-Control Laws After a Senator is Shot," U.S. News and World Report, LXXIV, February 12, 1973, 84.
Rohner, Ralph J. "Right to Bear Arms: A Phenomenon of Constitutional History," Catholic University Law Review, XVI, September 1966, 53.
Rolph, C. H. "Guns and Violence," New Statesman, LXIX, January 15, 1965, 71–72.
———. "Who Needs a Gun?" New Statesman, LXXIX, January 16, 1970, 70.
Rubin, S. "Cops, Guns and Homicides," Nation, CCI, December 27, 1965, 527–529.
"Run on Guns; A Lethal National Problem," Life, LIX, August 27, 1965, 59–61.
Russell, V. "Cruising Gun," Motor Boating and Sailing, CXL, October 1977, 54–55.
Safer, Jay Gerald. "Deadly Weapons in the Hands of Police Officers on Duty and Off Duty," Journal of Urban Law, XLIX, February 1972, 565+.
Samson, J. "Carter/Knox Team Wins a Big One; Handgun Debates at the Sixth Conference of Game Conservation International in San Antonio," Field nad Stream, LXXXII, September 1977, 41+.
———. "Editor; Harris Poll on Attitudes Towards Guns," Field and Stream, LXXXIII, November 1978, 4.
———. "Editorial; FAA Proposed Ban on Carrying Weapons in Airports," Field and Stream, LXXXII, September 1977, 4.
Sandys-Winsch, Godfrey. Gun Law. 2d ed. London: Shaw and Sons, 1973.
Schuman, H. and S. Presser. "Attitude Measurement and the Gun Control Paradox," Public Opinion Quarterly, XLI, Winter, 1977/1978, 527–438.
———. "The Gun Control Issues and Public Attitudes," Economic Outlook U.S.A., V. Summer, 1978, 54–55.

———. "Gun Registration," Society, XV, September 1978, 4.
Seitz, Stevan Thomas. "Firearms, Homicides, and Gun Control Effectiveness," Law and Society Review, VI, May 1972, 515–613.
Shaffer, Helen B. "Gun Control: Recurrent Issue," Editorial Research Reports, July 1972, 541-560.
Sheppard, Edward H. "Control of Fire Arms," Missouri Law Review, XXXIV, Summar, 1969, 376–396.
Sherrill, R. "High Noon On Capitol Hill; Each Year Americans Buy 3 Million More Guns," New York Times Magazine, June 23, 1968, 7–9.
———. "Lobby on Target," New York Times Magazine, October 15, 1967, 27+.
———. "Lobby on Target. Discussion," New York Times Magazine, November 5, 1967, 85; November 19, 1967, 42.
———. The Saturday Night Special, and Other Guns with which Americans Won the West, Protected Bootleg Franchises, Slew Wildlife, Robber Countless Banks, Shot Husbands Purposely and By Mistake, and Killed Presidents—Together with the Debate over Continuing the Same. New York: Charterhouse, 1973.
———. "Saturday Night Special and Other Hardware," New York Times Magazine, October 10, 1971, 15+.
———. "Saturday Night Special and Other Hardware. Discussion," New York Times Magazine, October 31, 1971, 54; November 21, 1971, 16+.
Sherrill, R. G. "Big Shoot; Gun-Restricting Legislation," Nation, XXII, March 7, 1966, 260–264.
Shield, J. "Why Nick," Newsweek, XCI, May 8, 1978, 23.
Shields, David J. and Marvin E. Aspen. "Two Judges Look at Gun Control," Chicago Bar Record, LVII, January/February 1976, 180–182+.
"Shot Down: Federal Control of Guns," Time, XIX, August 2, 1968, 19.
"Should Congress Pass Stronger Laws to Control Ownership of Guns?" Congressional Quarterly Weekly Report, XXXIII, April 1975, 798–799.
"Should the U.S. Ban the Handgun? 'No'," by Joseph M. Glaydos, American Legion Magazine, XCIX, September 1975, 14–15.
"Should We Worry About Gun Laws?" Economist, CCXLVII, May 12, 1973, 247.
"Small Expectations: Senate Gun-Control Hearings," Newsweek, LXX, July 24, 1967, 27.
Snyder, J. M. "Gun Law Enfeeblement; Reply," America, CXXII, January 31, 1970, 85.
Snyder, John M. "Crime Rises Under Rigid Gun Control," American Rifleman, CXVII, October 1969, 54–55.
"Sorry Gun Law," Economist, CCXXVII, June 8, 1968, 20.
South Dakota. State Legislative Research Council. Gun Control in South Dakota Including a Review of Federal and Other State Legislation; Informational Memorandum. Pierre: n.p., 1968.
Spiegler, Jeffrey H. and John Sweeny. Gun Abuse in Ohio. Cleveland: Administration of Justice Committee, an Affiliate of the Government Research Institute, 1975.
"Stalag in Kingston: Jamaica's Gun Court Act," Time, CIV, September 23, 1974, 55.
Stang, Alan. "American Liberty and Your Right to Your Gun," American Opinion, XXII, September 1979, 45–46+.
Stanton, Wettick, "The Effectiveness of State and Local Regulation of Handguns: A Statistical Analysis," Duke Law Journal, August 1969, 647–676.
Staples, Ernest L. and Richard T. Clayton. A Preliminary Cost Analysis of Firearms Control Programs, Prepared for National Commission on the Causes and Prevention of Violence. Silver Spring, Md.: Research Associates, 1968.
Starnes, R. "Anti-Gun Extremists are At It Again," Field and Stream, LXVIII, April 1964, 12+.
———. "Carter's Gun Bill: Controls and Hassles," October Life, CLXI, April 1978, 8+.
———. "Facts That Help You Fight for Hunting," Outdoor Life, CLXI, June 1978, 12+.
———. "Handbook for Arm Twisters; Letters to Legislators," Field and Stream, LXX, March 1966, 20+.
———. "High Noon in the Gun Battle," Field and Stream, LXX, June 1965, 12+.
———. "Honk's Life Insurance: Expert Marksmen Through Growing Up with Guns," Field and Stream, LXXI, November 1966, 16+.

———. "Law That Didn't Work;—Question of Crime Reduction by Massachusetts' Bartley-Fox Gun Law," Outdoor Life, CLVIII, December 1976, 10+.
———. "New Look at Gun Control," Outdoor Life, CLXIII, May 1979, 10+.
———. "No Time for Cheering, But . . .; Gun Control Controversy," Field and Stream, LXXX, February 1976, 12+.
Starnes, R. "147 Gun Laws," Field and Stream, CXXVII, February 1973, 8+.
———. "Philadelphia! Redtape Night-Mare," Field and Stream, LXXI, May 1966, 11–14+.
———. "Plot to Disarm Washington: Sullivan Law." Field and Stream, LXXVIII, September 1963, 18+.
———. "Pulling the Trigger Clause," Field and Stream, LXXX, June 1975, 10+.
———. "Son of Gangbusters: Treasury's Anti-Gun Film," Field and Stream, LXXIV, March 1970, 8+.
———. "Trash? Us? Comments on R. Sherrill's The Saturday Night Special," Field and Stream, LXXVIII, March 1974, 8+.
———. "You Might Call it CPS Distorts," Field and Stream, LXIX, September 1964, 20+.
———. "Your Firearms and the Plan to Take Them," Field and Stream, LXXII, June 1967, 12–13+.
——— and T. J. Dodd. "Your Right to Own a Gun; Pro and Con Discussion," Popular Mechanics, CXXI, February 1964, 94–99+.
"State Legislature Activity—1965," American Rifleman, September, 1965, 24.
Stolley, R. "Spy Among the Minutemen," Life, LIX, July 2, 1965, 40D.
Stuart, P. C. "Shooting Down Gun Control," New Leader, LXI, September 11, 1978, 7–9.
———. "Shooting Down Gun Control. Reply with Rejoinder," by W. S. Booth, New Leader, LXI, November 20, 1978, 27.
"Taming Our Violence," Commonweal, CII, October 10, 1975, 451–452.
"Teacher Opinion Poll; Gun Control Legislation," Today's Education, LXIX. January 1970, 11.
Terry, W. "Handgun Menace," Progressive, XLIII, February 1979, 12.
"This Month's Feature: Congress and Gun Control Proposals," Congressional Digest, XLV, December 1966, 289–314.
"This Month's Feature: Congress and the National Crime Problem," Congressional Digest, XLVI, August 1967, 193–224.
"This Month's Feature: Controversy Over Proposed Federal Handgun Controls," Congressional Digest, LIV, December 1975, 289–314.
"Tighter Gun Controls, Both Sides of the Dispute; Symposium," U.S. News and World Report, LXXIII, July 10, 1972, 68–70.
"Time to Ban Handguns," Progressive, XLI, January 1977, 10–11.
"Time to Control the Gun Trade," America, CXXVI, June 17, 1972, 625.
Toynbee, Polly, "Shooting Down Some Myths" Washington Monthly, V, December 1973, 24–31.
"TRB From Washington," New Republic, CLXXX, February 10, 1979, 3.
"TRB From Washington: Bang, Bang," New Republic, CLXXIII, September 20, 1975.
"TRB From Washington: Who's Guilty?" New Republic, CLVIII, June 15, 1968, 2.
"Triggered," Economist, CCLV, April 1975, 72–74.
Trueblood, T. "Nampa Story: Work of Nampa, Idaho, Rod and Gun Club," Field and Stream, LXXX, February 1976, 22+.
United States, Comptroller General. Handgun Control: Effectiveness and Costs. Washington, D.C.: n.p., 1978.
United States. Congress. House. Committee on Post Office and Civil Service. Subcommittee on Postal Operations. Mail Order Gun Control. Hearing on H.R. 17949, July 2, 1968. 90th Congress, 2d Session, Washington, 1968.
United States. Congress. House. Committee on the District of Columbia. Firearms Control Regulations Act of 1975, Council Act No. 1–142. Hearing and Disposition on H. Con. Res. 694, August 25, 1976. 94th Congress, 2d Session, Washington, D.C., 1976.
United States. Congress. House. Committee on the Judiciary. Subcommittee No. 5. Gun Control Legislation. Hearings on H.R. 8828 and Related Bills, June 27, 28 and 29, 1972. 92d Congress, 2d Session, Washington, D.C., 1972.
United States. Congress. House. Committee on the Judiciary. Subcommittee on Crime. Firearms Legislation. Hearings, February 8–June 23, 1975. 94th Congress, 1st Session, Washington, D.C., 1975.

———. Organized Crime Control Act of 1970. Hearings on S. 1083, November 26, 1974. 93d Congress, 2d Session. Washington, D.C., 1974.
———. Treasury's Proposed Gun Regulations. Hearings, May 4 and 18, 1978. 95th Congress, 2d Session, Washington, D.C., 1979.
United States. Congress. House. Committee on Ways and Means. Proposed Amendments to Firearms Acts. Hearings, July 12–28, 1965. 89th Congress, 1st Session, Washington, D.C., 1965.
United States. Congress. House. Conference Committees, 1968. Gun Control Act of 1968, Conference Report to Accompany H.R. 17735. 90th Congress, 2d Session, Washington, D.C., 1968. (House of Representatives Report No. 1956).
United States. Congress. Senate. Committee on Commerce. Interstate Shipment of Firearms. Hearing on S. 1975, a Bill to Amend the Federal Firearms Act and S. 2345, a Bill to Amend the Federal Firearms Act to Further Restrict the Use of Instrumentalities of Interstate or Foreign Commerce for the Acquisition of Firearms for Unlawful Purposes, December 13, 1963–March 4, 1964. 88th Congress, 2d Session, Washington, D.C., 1964.
United States. Congress. Senate. Committee on Government Operations. Permanent Subcommittee on Investigations. Illicit Traffic in Weapons and Drugs Across the United States–Mexican Border. Hearing, January 12, 1977. 95th Congress, 1st Session, Washington, D.C., 1977.
United States. Congress. Senate. Commerce on the Judiciary. Gun Control Act of 1968, Report Together With Individual Views to Accompany S. 3633, 90th Congress, Washington, D.C., 1968. (Senate Report No. 1501).
———. Subcommittee to Investigate Juvenile Delinquency. Federal Firearms Act. Hearings on S. Res. 52. 89th Congress, 1st Session, Washington, D.C., 1965.
———. Federal Firearms Act. Hearings on S. Res. 35. 90th Congress, 1st Session, Washington, D.C., 1967.
———. Federal Firearms Legislation. Hearings on S. Res. 240, S. 3691 and Other Bills, June 26–July 10, 1968, 90th Congress, 2d Session, Washington, D.C., 1968.
———. Firearms Legislation. Hearings on S. Res. 48, July 23, 24, and 29, 1969. 91st Congress, 1st Session, Washington, D.C., 1970.
———. Handgun Crime Control, 1975–1976. Hearings on S. Res. 72, April 23, July 22, October 28, 1975. 94th Congress, 1st Session, Washington, D.C., 1976.
———. Interstate Traffic in Mail Order Firearms, Interim Report with Individual Views Pursuant to S. Res. 274, August 7, 1964. 88th Congress, 2d Session, Washington, D.C., 1964. (Senate Report No. 1340).
———. Juvenile Delinquency. Hearings on S. Res. 274, March 26–April 25, 1964. 88th Congress, 2d Session, Washington, D.C., 1964.
———. "Saturday Night Special" Handguns. Hearings on S. 2507, September 13–November 1, 1971. 92d Congress, 1st Session, Washington, D.C., 1972.
United States. Library of Congress. Congressional Research Service. Combating Crime in the United States. Selected Excerpts and References Relating to the National Debats Topic for American High Schools, 1967–1968, Pursuant to Public Law 88–246. Washington, D.C.: GPO, 1967.
———. Federal Gun Control. Washington, D.C.: GPO, 1973.
———. Gun Control in the United States; Selected References. Washington, D.C.: GPO, 1972.
———. Gun Control: The Constitutionality of Federal Prohibitions on the Mere Possession of Firearms as an Exercise of the Commerce Power. Washington, D.C.: GPO, 1975.
United States. Treasury Department. Bureau of Alcohol, Tobacco and Firearms. Alcohol, Tobacco and Firearms Bulletin. Washington, D.C.: GPO, 1974.
———. Alcohol, Tobacco and Firearms Bulletin. Washington, D.C.: GPO, 1975.
———. Concentrated Urban Enforcement: An Analysis of the Initial Year of Operation CUE in the Cities of Washington, D.C., Boston, Mass., Chicago, Ill. Washington, D.C.: The Bureau, 1977.
———. Federal Regulation of Firearms and Ammunition. Washington, D.C.: The Bureau, 1978.
———. Published Ordinances Firearms; State Laws and Local Ordinances Relevant to Title 18, U.S.C., Chapter 44. Washington, D.C.: The Bureau, 1972. (United States. Internal Revenue Service. Publication 603.)
———. Your 1976 Guide to Firearms Regulations. Washington, D.C.: The Bureau, 1976.

United States. Treasury Department. Interstate Traffic in Firearms and Ammunition (Federal Firearms Act), Part 177 of Title 26, Code of Federal Regulations, Rev. Washington, D.C.: GPO, 1965. (United States. Treasury Department, Publication No. 417.)
"Use of Prior Uncounseled Convictions in Federal Gun Control Prosecutions," Harvard Law Review, XCII, June 1979, 1790–1800.
"Veto Coming? Anticrime Program in Senate," Newsweek, LXXI, May 27, 1968, 33B–34.
Wassermann, M. "Gun Law Failure; Massachusetts' Bartley-Fox Law," Progressive, XI, April 1976, 32–33.
Weatherup, Roy G. "Standing Armies and Armed Citizens: An Historical Analysis of the Second Amendment," Hasting's Constitutional Law Quarterly, II, Fall 1975, 961–1001.
Weber, P. J. "National Rifle Association: Public Enemy No. 2," Christian Century, XCI, October 16, 1974, 953–960.
Weil, D. "Right to Bear Arms," Atlantic, CCXXXIX, February 1977, 64–67.
Weiss, Jonathan A. "A Reply to Advocates of Gun-Control Law," Journal of Urban Law, LII, Winter, 1975, 577–589.
"What Congress is Doing to Curb Sales of Guns and Ammunition," U.S. News and World Report, LXV, August 5, 1968, 8.
"What Other Nations Do About Guns," U.S. News and World Report, LV, December 23 1963 71.
Whisker, James B. The Citizen Soldier and U.S. Military Policy. Thornwood, N.Y.: Caroline House, 1979.
———. "Historical Development and Subsequent Erosion of the Right to Keep and Bear Arms," West Virginia Law Review, LXXVIII, February, 1976, 171–190.
———. Our Vanishing Freedom; The Right to Keep and Bear Arms. McLean, Va.: Heritage House, 1972.
"Who Needs an Antitank Gun? Need for Control Bill," Life, LXII, January 13, 1967, 6.
"Why Arm Potential Killers?" Saturday Evening Post, CCXXXV, October 6, 1962, 98.
Williams, J. Sherwood and John H. McGrath. "Why People Own Guns," Journal of Communication, XXVI, Autumn, 1976, 22–30.
"Win for the Gun Lobby," Newsweek, LXX, September 4, 1967, 29–30.
Wisconsin. Legislative Assembly. Committee on State Affairs. Report on Gun Control Legislation and "Stop and Frisk" Laws. Madison: n.p., 1968.
Wright, J. D. "Demography of Gun Control," Nation, CCXXI, September 20, 1975, 240–244.
———. "Who Owns the Side Arms? The Demography of Gun Control," Nation, CCXXI, September 20, 1975, 240–244.
——— and Linda L. Marston. "Ownership of the Means of Destruction: Weapons in the United States," Social Problems, XXIII, October 1975, 93–107.
Yeager, Matthew G. Do Mandatory Prison Sentences for Handgun Offenders Curb Violent Crime? 2d ed, rev. Washington, D.C.: United States Conference of Mayors, 1976. (Technical Report. United States Conference of Mayors; 1).
Zimring, F. E. "Firearms and Federal Law: The Gun Control Act of 1968," Journal of Legal Studies, IV, January 1975, 133–198.
———. "Games With Guns and Statistics," Wisconsin Law Review, 1968, 1113–1126.
———. "Getting Serious About Guns," Nation, CCXIV, April 10, 1972, 457–461.
———. "Is Gun Control Likely to Reduce Violent Killings?" University of Chicago Law Review, XXXV, Summer 1968, 721–737.
———. "Hard Choices," Trial, VIII, January/February 1972, 52+.

Appendix

DEPARTMENT OF THE TREASURY
BUREAU OF ALCOHOL, TOBACCO AND FIREARMS
APPLICATION FOR LICENSE
UNDER 18 U.S.C. Chapter 44, FIREARMS

FOR ATF USE ONLY

FOR INTERNAL REVENUE SERVICE CENTER USE ONLY

1. NAME OF OWNER OR CORPORATION *(If partnership, include name of each partner)*

2. TRADE OR BUSINESS NAME, IF ANY

3. EMPLOYER IDENTIFICATION NUMBER OR SOCIAL SECURITY NO

4. NAME OF COUNTY IN WHICH BUSINESS IS LOCATED

5. BUSINESS ADDRESS *(RFD or street no., city, state, zip code)*

6. BUSINESS LOCATION *(If no street address in item 5, show directions & distance from nearest P.O. or city limits)*

7. TELEPHONE NUMBER *(Include Area Code)*
BUSINESS ______
RESIDENCE ______

8. APPLICANT'S BUSINESS IS
☐ INDIVIDUALLY OWNED ☐ A CORPORATION
☐ A PARTNERSHIP ☐ OTHER *(Specify)* ______

9. APPLICANT'S BUSINESS IS LOCATED IN
☐ A COMMERCIAL BUILDING ☐ A RESIDENCE *(See instruction 4)*
☐ OTHER *(Specify)* ______

10. IS ANY BUSINESS OTHER THAN THAT FOR WHICH THE LICENSE APPLICATION IS BEING MADE CONDUCTED ON THE BUSINESS PREMISES *(If "Yes" give the general nature of that business)*
☐ YES ☐ NO

11. DATE APPLICANT DESIRES TO COMMENCE BUSINESS REQUIRING A LICENSE

12. APPLICATION IS MADE FOR A LICENSE UNDER 18 U.S.C. CHAPTER 44 AS A: *(Place and (X) in column (b) of the appropriate line. Submit the fee shown in column (c) with the application.)*

	TYPE OF LICENSE a	"X" b	FEE c
1	DEALER IN FIREARMS OTHER THAN DESTRUCTIVE DEVICES OR AMMUNITION FOR OTHER THAN DESTRUCTIVE DEVICES *(INCLUDES Rifles, Shotguns, Pistols, Revolvers, Ammunition only, Gunsmith activities and National Firearms Act (NFA) Weapons)*		$10
2	PAWNBROKER DEALING IN FIREARMS OTHER THAN DESTRUCTIVE DEVICES OR AMMUNITION FOR FIREARMS OTHER THAN DESTRUCTIVE DEVICES		$25
3	COLLECTOR OF CURIOS AND RELICS *(Note: Omit items 14 and 15 if checked here and no other licenses are applied for.)*		$10
6	MANUFACTURER OF AMMUNITION FOR FIREARMS OTHER THAN DESTRUCTIVE DEVICES		$10
7	MANUFACTURER OF FIREARMS OTHER THAN DESTRUCTIVE DEVICES		$50
8	IMPORTER OF FIREARMS OTHER THAN DESTRUCTIVE DEVICES OR AMMUNITION FOR FIREARMS OTHER THAN DESTRUCTIVE DEVICES *		$50
9	DEALER IN DESTRUCTIVE DEVICES OR AMMUNITION FOR DESTRUCTIVE DEVICES *		$1000
10	MANUFACTURER OF DESTRUCTIVE DEVICES OR AMMUNITION FOR DESTRUCTIVE DEVICES *		$1000
11	IMPORTER OF DESTRUCTIVE DEVICES OR AMMUNITION FOR DESTRUCTIVE DEVICES		$1000

Note; Applicants intending to engage in businesses relating to NFA weapons (including destructive devices and ammunition for destructive devices) are required to pay a special (occupational) tax before commencing business (26 USC 5801).

13. PAYMENT FOR THE LICENSE, MADE PAYABLE TO THE INTERNAL REVENUE SERVICE IS ATTACHED OR ENCLOSED IN THE FORM OF: ☐ CHECK ☐ MONEY ORDER ☐ OTHER *(Specify)* ______ AMOUNT SUBMITTED $

14. HOURS OF OPERATION APPLICANT'S BUSINESS

TIME	SUNDAY	MONDAY	TUESDAY	WEDNESDAY	THURSDAY	FRIDAY	SATURDAY
OPEN							
CLOSE							

15. ARE THE APPLICANT'S BUSINESS PREMISES OPEN TO THE GENERAL PUBLIC DURING THESE HOURS
☐ YES
☐ NO *(If no, give explanation on separate sheet)*

16. IS APPLICANT PRESENTLY ENGAGED IN A BUSINESS REQUIRING A FEDERAL FIREARMS LICENSE *(If yes, answer 17 to 21)*
☐ YES ☐ NO

17. APPROXIMATELY HOW MANY FIREARMS WERE SOLD BY APPLICANT DURING THE PRECEDING TWELVE MONTHS

18. PRESENT LICENSE NUMBER

19. DATE FIREARM BUSINESS COMMENCED

IF BUSINESS OBTAINED FROM SOMEONE ELSE GIVE

20. NAME

21. LICENSE NUMBER

ATF Form 7 (5310.12) (11-77) PREVIOUS EDITIONS ARE OBSOLETE

SERVICE CENTER

22 DESCRIBE SPECIFIC ACTIVITY APPLICANT IS ENGAGED IN, OR INTENDS TO ENGAGE IN, WHICH WILL REQUIRE A FEDERAL FIREARMS LICENSE
(e.g. dealer in rifles, shotguns, revolvers and ammunition, dealer in ammunition only, gunsmith, dealer in machine guns, etc.)

23 IS STATE OF LOCAL LICENSE OR PERMIT REQUIRED FOR APPLICANT'S BUSINESS? *(If "yes," give numbers or if not obtained, date applied for.)*

☐ YES ☐ NO

24 LIST BELOW THE INFORMATION REQUIRED FOR EACH INDIVIDUAL OWNER, PARTNER AND OTHER RESPONSIBLE PERSONS *(see Instruction 7)* IN THE APPLICANT BUSINESS. IF A FEMALE, LIST GIVEN NAMES AND MAIDEN, IF MARRIED, e.g., "MARY ALICE (SMITH) JONES," NOT "MRS JOHN JONES"
(If additional space is needed use a separate sheet.)

FULL NAME	POSITION AND SOCIAL SECURITY NO	HOME ADDRESS *(Include Zip Code)*	PLACE OF BIRTH	DATE OF BIRTH

25 HAS APPLICANT OR ANY PERSON LISTED ABOVE *(If "Yes," place an (*) by the name and show the city and state at right)*	YES	NO	
A HELD A FEDERAL FIREARMS LICENSE			CITY
B BEEN DENIED A FEDERAL FIREARMS LICENSE			
C BEEN AN OFFICER IN A CORPORATION HOLDING A FEDERAL FIREARMS LICENSE			STATE
D BEEN AN EMPLOYEE RESPONSIBLE FOR FIREARMS ACTIVITIES OF A FEDERAL FIREARMS LICENSE			

GIVE FULL DETAILS ON SEPARATE SHEET FOR ALL "Yes" ANSWERS IN ITEMS 26 & 27.		YES	NO
26 IS APPLICANT OR ANY PERSON NAMED IN ITEM 24 ABOVE	A CHARGED BY INFORMATION OR UNDER INDICTMENT IN ANY COURT FOR A CRIME PUNISHABLE BY IMPRISONMENT FOR A TERM EXCEEDING ONE YEAR		
	B A FUGITIVE FROM JUSTICE		
	C AN ALIEN WHO IS ILLEGALLY OR UNLAWFULLY IN THE UNITED STATES		
	D UNDER 21 YEARS OF AGE		
	E AN UNLAWFUL USER OF OR ADDICTED TO MARIHUANA OR ANY DEPRESSANT, STIMULANT OR NARCOTIC DRUG		
27 HAS APPLICANT OR ANY PERSON NAMED IN ITEM 24 EVER	A BEEN CONVICTED IN ANY COURT OF A CRIME PUNISHABLE BY IMPRISONMENT FOR A TERM EXCEEDING ONE YEAR *(See 1 below)*		
	B BEEN DISCHARGED FROM THE ARMED FORCES UNDER DISHONORABLE CONDITIONS		
	C BEEN ADJUDICATED AS A MENTAL DEFECTIVE OR BEEN COMMITTED TO ANY MENTAL INSTITUTION		
	D RENOUNCED HIS CITIZENSHIP, HAVING BEEN A CITIZEN OF THE UNITED STATES		

28 **CERTIFICATION**. Under the penalties imposed by 18 U.S.C. 924, I declare that I have examined this application and the documents submitted in support thereof, and to the best of my knowledge and belief, they are true, correct and complete

SIGN HERE ▶	TITLE	DATE

FOR ATF USE

29 APPLICATION IS	*(Give reasons for terminated or disapproved application)*	
☐ APPROVED ☐ DISAPPROVED* ☐ TERMINATED* * LICENSE FEE WILL BE REFUNDED BY INTERNAL REVENUE SERVICE		
SIGNATURE OF REGIONAL REGULATORY ADMINISTRATOR		DATE

1/(The actual sentence given by the judge does not matter - a "yes" answer is necessary if the judge could have given a sentence of more than one year. Also, a "yes" answer is required even if a conviction has been discharged, set aside, or dismissed pursuant to an expungement or rehabilitation statute.)

ATF Form 7 (5310.12) (11-77)

1. Name

2. License Number	3. Expiration Date

5. Type of License ____________

01 Dealer in firearms other than destructive devices or ammunition for other than destructive devices (Fee $10)

02 Pawnbroker dealing in firearms other than destructive devices or ammunition for firearms other than destructive devices (Fee $25)

03 Collector of curios and relics (Fee $10)

06 Manufacturer of ammunition for firearms other than destructive devices. (Fee $10)

07 Manufacturer of firearms other than destructive devices. (Fee $50)

08 Importer of firearms other than destructive devices or ammunition for firearms other than destructive devices. (Fee $50)

09 Dealer in destructive devices or ammunition for destructive devices. (Fee $1000)

10 Manufacturer of destructive devices or ammunition for destructive devices. (Fee $1000)

11 Importer of destructive devices or ammunition for destructive devices. (Fee $1000)

4. Issued by Regional Regulatory Administrator, ATF, at (Address)

6. Correct any errors in this space

ATF Form 8 (5310.11) PART III (3-80) EDITION OF 6-79 MAY BE USED

RENEWAL OF FIREARMS LICENSE

If you want to renew your firearms license, you MUST do the following before the expiration date shown at the left:

1. Examine the front of this form. If there are errors, please cross out the wrong information and write the correct information in the lower left-hand corner.

2. FILL OUT THE BACK OF THIS FORM AND SIGN IT.

3. Make check or money order payable to Internal Revenue Service.

4. Mail the completed form and required fee (shown at the left) in the enclosed envelope.

WARNING: There are criminal penalties for continuing your firearms business without renewing your license.

DEPARTMENT OF THE TREASURY – BUREAU OF ALCOHOL, TOBACCO AND FIREARMS

The following questions apply to you and (if the licensee is a corporation, partnership or association) to any other person who has the power to direct the management and policies of your firearms business.

Yes	No	
☐	☐	1. Are you actively engaged in the firearms or ammunition business (or collecting activity) authorized by this license?
☐	☐	2. Are you presently under indictment or information in any court for a crime punishable by imprisonment for a term exceeding 1 year? (If yes, attach an explanatory statement showing the date of the indictment or information and the court in which it is pending. "Information" means a formal accusation of a crime made by a prosecuting attorney as distinguished from an indictment presented by a grand jury.)
☐	☐	3. Have you ever been convicted of a crime punishable by imprisonment for a term exceeding 1 year?
☐	☐	4. Are you presently appealing a conviction of a crime punishable by imprisonment for a term exceeding 1 year? (If yes, attach an explanatory statement showing date of conviction, court in which convicted and court in which appeal is pending)

NOTE: For questions 2, 3, and 4, the actual sentence given by the judge does not matter. You must answer yes if the Judge could have given a sentence of imprisonment for more than 1 year. Also, a yes answer is required (1) if you received probation, (2) if the conviction was discharged or set aside, (3) if the conviction was dismissed under an expungement or rehabilitation statute, or (4) if the conviction was appealed. However, a crime punishable by imprisonment for a term exceeding 1 year does not include a conviction which has been set aside under the Federal Youth Corrections Act.

Yes	No	
☐	☐	5. Are you a fugitive from justice?
☐	☐	6. Are you an unlawful user of, or addicted to marihuana or any depressant, stimulant or narcotic drug?
☐	☐	7. Have you ever been adjudicated mentally defective, mentally incompetent or been committed to a mental institution?
☐	☐	8. Have you been discharged from the Armed Forces under dishonorable conditions?
☐	☐	9. Are you an alien illegally or unlawfully in the United States?
☐	☐	10 Have you ever renounced your United States citizenship?
☐	☐	11 Has there been a change of the ownership or control of the firearms business?

Under the penalties imposed by 18 U.S.C. 924, I certify that the statements contained in this application are true and correct to the best of my knowledge and belief.

Signature_______________________________Date __________

Title ____
(owner, partner or officer of a corporation)

ATF Forms 8 (5310.11) PART III (3-80)

1 Name	
2 License Number	3 Expiration Date
5 Type of License ______ 01 Dealer in firearms other than destructive devices or ammunition for other than destructive devices 02 Pawnbroker dealing in firearms other than destructive devices or ammunition for firearms other than destructive devices 03 Collector of curios and relics 06 Manufacturer of ammunition for firearms other than destructive devices 07 Manufacturer of firearms other than destructive devices	08 Importer of firearms other than destructive devices or ammunition for firearms other than destructive devices 09 Dealer in destructive devices or ammunition for destructive devices 10 Manufacturer of destructive devices or ammunition for destructive devices 11 Importer of destructive devices or ammunition for destructive devices
4 Issued by Regional Regulatory Administrator, ATF at (Address)	
6 Signature of Regional Regulatory Administrator	

ATF Form 8 (5310.11) (5-80) PART 1 EDITION of 5-78 MAY BE USED

License (18 U.S.C. Chapter 44)

In accordance with the provisions of Title 1, Gun Control Act of 1968, and the regulations issued thereunder (27 CFR Part 178), you are licensed to engage in the business specified in item 5 of the license, within the limitations of Chapter 44, Title 18, United States Code, and the regulations issued thereunder, until the expiration date specified in item 3 of this license. See "WARNING" on back.

Department of the Treasury
Bureau of Alcohol, Tobacco and Firearms

Please include your license number on all correspondence with the Bureau.

WARNING

This license is not a permit to carry a concealed weapon nor does it confer the right or privilege to conduct business contrary to State law or any other law. Whenever a person who possesses a license under 18 U.S.C. Chapter 44 becomes a fugitive from justice; becomes addicted to marihuana or any depressant, stimulant, or narcotic drug; is adjudicated as a mental defective or is committed to a mental institution; has been discharged from the Armed Forces under dishonorable conditions; renounces his citizenship or, except as provided in 18 U.S.C. 925 and Title VII of Public Law 90-351 (82 Stat. 197) (18 U.S.C. App.), is finally convicted of a crime punishable by imprisonment for a term exceeding one year, such person is prohibited from engaging in the business otherwise authorized by this license.

NOTICE

Any changes in name, trade name, address, or control of this business must be reported PROMPTLY to the Regional Regulatory Administrator, Bureau of Alcohol, Tobacco and Firearms from whom this license was received. Failure to do so may result in administrative action against the licensee for failure to comply with applicable regulations. (27 CFR 178.52 - 178.54)

Any person who fails to make application for renewal of this license prior to expiration of this license is also prohibited from engaging in the business presently authorized. If a renewal application is not received 30 days before the expiration date, the licensee should contact his Regional Regulatory Administrator concerning renewal. (27 CFR 178.45)

This license is conditional upon compliance by you with the Clean Water Act.

1 Name

2 License Number | 3 Expiration Date

5 Type of License

01 Dealer in firearms other than destructive devices or ammunition for other than destructive devices

02 Pawnbroker dealing in firearms other than destructive devices or ammunition for firearms other than destructive devices

03 Collector of curios and relics

06 Manufacturer of ammunition for firearms other than destructive devices

07 Manufacturer of firearms other than destructive devices

08 Importer of firearms other than destructive devices or ammunition for firearms other than destructive devices

09 Dealer in destructive devices or ammunition for destructive devices

10 Manufacturer of destructive devices or ammunition for destructive devices

11 Importer of destructive devices or ammunition for destructive devices

4 Issued by Regional Regulatory Administrator, ATF at (Address)

6 Signature of Regional Regulatory Administrator

ATF Form 8 (5310.11) (5-80) PART II

Copy of License (18 U.S.C. Chapter 44)

I certify that this is a true copy of a license issued to me to engage in the business specified in item 5.

(Signature of Licensee)

PURCHASING COPY

The licensee named herein may use this form, a reproduction thereof, or a reproduction of his license, to assist a transferor of firearms to verify the identity and the licensed status of the licensee as provided in 27 CFR Part 178

DEPARTMENT OF THE TREASURY — BUREAU OF ALCOHOL, TOBACCO AND FIREARMS

1 Name

2 License Number | 3 Expiration Date

5 Type of License

01 Dealer in firearms other than destructive devices or ammunition for other than destructive devices

02 Pawnbroker dealing in firearms other than destructive devices or ammunition for firearms other than destructive devices

03 Collector of curios and relics

06 Manufacturer of ammunition for firearms other than destructive devices

07 Manufacturer of firearms other than destructive devices

08 Importer of firearms other than destructive devices or ammunition for firearms other than destructive devices

09 Dealer in destructive devices or ammunition for destructive devices

10 Manufacturer of destructive devices or ammunition for destructive devices

11 Importer of destructive devices or ammunition for destructive devices

4 Issued by Regional Regulatory Administrator, ATF at (Address)

6 Signature of Regional Regulatory Administrator

ATF Form 8 (5310.11) (5-80) PART IV

Record Copy of License (18 U.S.C. Chapter 44)

In accordance with the provisions of Title 1, Gun Control Act of 1968, and the regulations issued thereunder (27 CFR Part 178), you are licensed to engage in the business specified in item 5 of the license, within the limitations of Chapter 44, Title 18, United States Code, and the regulations issued thereunder, until the expiration date specified in item 3 of this license.

Department of the Treasury
Bureau of Alcohol, Tobacco and Firearms

DEPARTMENT OF THE TREASURY — BUREAU OF ALCOHOL, TOBACCO AND FIREARMS

1 Name

2 License Number	3 Expiration Date

5 Type of License

01 Dealer in firearms other than destructive devices or ammunition for other than destructive devices

02 Pawnbroker dealing in firearms other than destructive devices or ammunition for firearms other than destructive devices

03 Collector of curios and relics

06 Manufacturer of ammunition for firearms other than destructive devices

07 Manufacturer of firearms other than destructive devices

08 Importer of firearms other than destructive devices or ammunition for firearms other than destructive devices

09 Dealer in destructive devices or ammunition for destructive devices

10 Manufacturer of destructive devices or ammunition for destructive devices

11 Importer of destructive devices or ammunition for destructive devices

4 Issued by Regional Regulatory Administrator ATF at (Address)

6 Signature of Regional Regulatory Administrator

ATF Form 8 (5310 11) (5-80) PART V

Record Copy of License (18 U.S.C. Chapter 44)

In accordance with the provisions of Title 1, Gun Control Act of 1968, and the regulations issued thereunder (27 CFR Part 178), you are licensed to engage in the business specified in item 5 of the license, within the limitations of Chapter 44, Title 18, United States Code, and the regulations issued thereunder, until the expiration date specified in item 3 of this license.

Department of the Treasury
Bureau of Alcohol, Tobacco and Firearms

DEPARTMENT OF THE TREASURY — BUREAU OF ALCOHOL, TOBACCO AND FIREARMS

1 Name

2 License Number	3 Expiration Date

5 Type of License

01 Dealer in firearms other than destructive devices or ammunition for other than destructive devices

02 Pawnbroker dealing in firearms other than destructive devices or ammunition for firearms other than destructive devices

03 Collector of curios and relics

06 Manufacturer of ammunition for firearms other than destructive devices

07 Manufacturer of firearms other than destructive devices

08 Importer of firearms other than destructive devices or ammunition for firearms other than destructive devices

09 Dealer in destructive devices or ammunition for destructive devices

10 Manufacturer of destructive devices or ammunition for destructive devices

11 Importer of destructive devices or ammunition for destructive devices

4 Issued by Regional Regulatory Administrator, ATF at (Address)

6 Signature of Regional Regulatory Administrator

ATF Form 8 (5310 11) (5-80) PART VI

Record Copy of License (18 U.S.C. Chapter 44)

In accordance with the provisions of Title 1, Gun Control Act of 1968, and the regulations issued thereunder (27 CFR Part 178), you are licensed to engage in the business specified in item 5 of the license, within the limitations of Chapter 44, Title 18, United States Code, and the regulations issued thereunder, until the expiration date specified in item 3 of this license.

Department of the Treasury
Bureau of Alcohol, Tobacco and Firearms

DEPARTMENT OF THE TREASURY — BUREAU OF ALCOHOL, TOBACCO AND FIREARMS

RECORD OF INSPECTION ASSIGNMENTS AND REPORTS	TELE. NO. & AREA CODE	HRS. OF OPN	SUN	MON	TUE	WED	THU	FRI	SAT
	BUS	OPEN							
	RES.	CLOSE							

ASSIGNMENTS			REPORTS		
DATE	TYPE	INSPECTORS	DATE	TIME 1/	VIOLATIONS, SUMMATIONS, REFERRALS, AND RECOMMENDATIONS

1/ *Total spent on the inspection, including report writing but excluding travel*

DEPARTMENT OF THE TREASURY
BUREAU OF ALCOHOL, TOBACCO AND FIREARMS

APPLICATION FOR LICENSE

UNDER 18 U.S.C. Chapter 44, FIREARMS

INSTRUCTION SHEET FOR ATF FORM 7

(Detach this instruction sheet before submitting your application)

1. Please read carefully before preparing AFT Form 7. Issuance of your license under 18 U.S.C. Chapter 44 will be delayed if form submitted is incomplete or otherwise improperly prepared. This application should be submitted in sufficient time to reach the Internal Revenue Service Center at least 45 days in advance of the date that the license is required.

2. Submit an original and one copy of ATF Form 7 to the Director, Internal Revenue Service Center, at the address shown below for the State in which the applicant's business is to be conducted. (CAUTION: Submission of this application does NOT authorize the applicant to engage in any of the activities covered by the requested license. A license must be received before operations are commenced.)

3. Print with ball point pen or typewriter. If separate sheets are needed they must be:

   a. Submitted in duplicate.
   b. Identified with your name and address at the top of the page.
   c. Referenced by the question number being expanded.

4. A license will not be issued to an applicant who intends to conduct his firearms business from a private residence unless his firearms business premises are accessible to the public, i.e., the clientele that the business is set up to serve. If a license is issued, ATF officers will have access to the firearms business premises during business hours and such access includes ingress to the non-public portion of the residence if necessary.

5. A license will not be issued to an applicant who does not intend to actually engage in the firearms activity covered by the license applied for.

6. License fees are to be paid at the time application is made. Make checks or money orders payable to the Internal Revenue Service. Insert your employer identification number or social security number on the check or money order. The actual fee is determined by the type license sought. (*See item 12 on ATF Form 7 for correct fees.*)

   a. Multiple License — An applicant can apply for a multiple license by checking more than 1 category in item 12, provided that the fee for each activity is paid and the business is conducted at the same location.

   b. Multiple Locations — A separate application and license fee is required for the business at each location.

7. Responsible Persons — As used in item 24, means:

   a. In the case of a corporation, partnership, or association, any individual possessing, directly or indirectly, the power to direct or cause the direction of the management, policies, and buying and selling practices of the corporation, partnership, or association, insofar as such management, policies and buying and selling practices pertain to firearms or ammunition, and

   b. In the case of a corporation, association, or similar organization, any person owning ten percent or more of the outstanding shares of stock issued by the applicant business, and

   c. In the case of a corporation, association, or similar organization, the officers and directors thereof.

8. The certification in item 28 must be executed on the original and copy of ATF Form 7 by the owner, a partner, or in the case of a corporation, association, etc., by an officer duly authorized to sign for the applicant.

9. If you have any questions relating to this application, please contact the appropriate Bureau of Alcohol, Tobacco and Firearms office listed on the reverse.

10. The Regional Regulatory Administrator (ATF) in your geographical area will: (1) issue a license if your application is approved; (2) advise you in writing of the reasons for denial of application. Fees will be returned for application denied.

IF APPLICANT'S BUSINESS IS TO BE CONDUCTED IN:	MAIL TO: DIRECTOR INTERNAL REVENUE SERVICE CENTER
Guam, New Jersey, New York City and counties of Nassau, Rockland Suffolk, and Westchester	1040 Waverly Avenue Holtsville, N.Y. 11799* *Use 00501 After 1-1-78
New York (*all other counties*), Connecticut, Maine, Massachusetts, New Hampshire, Rhode Island, Vermont	310 Lowell Street Andover, Mass. 01812* *Use 05501 After 1-1-78
District of Columbia, Delaware, Maryland, Pennsylvania	11601 Roosevelt Boulevard Philadelphia, Pa. 19155* *Use 19255 After 1-1-78
Alabama, Flordia, Georgia, Mississippi, South Carolina	4800 Buford Highway Chamblee, Georgia 30006* *Use 31101 After 1-1-78
Michigan, Ohio	Cincinnati, Ohio 45298* *Use 45999 After 1-1-78

IF APPLICANT'S BUSINESS IS TO BE CONDUCTED IN:	MAIL TO: DIRECTOR INTERNAL REVENUE SERVICE CENTER
Arkansas, Kansas, Louisiana, New Mexico, Oklahoma, Texas	3651 S. Interregional Hwy. Austin, Texas 78740* *Use 73301 After 1-1-78
Alaska, Arizona, Colorado, Idaho, Minnesota, Montana, Nebraska, Nevada, North Dakota, Oregon, South Dekota, Utah, Washington, Wyoming	1160 West 1200 South St. Ogden, Utah 84201
Illinois, Iowa, Missouri, Wisconsin	2306 E. Bannister Road Kansas City, Mo. 64170* *Use 64999 After 1-1-78
California, Hawaii	5045 East Butler Avenue Fresno, California 93888
Indiana, Kentucky, North Carolina, Tennessee, Virginia, West Virginia	3131 Democrat Road Memphis, Tennessee 38110* *Use 37501 After 1-1-78

DETACH INSTRUCTIONS BEFORE FILING

Index to Cases

Subject Index

About the Author

WARREN FREEDMAN was formerly Counsel and Assistant Secretary for Bristol-Myers Co. His previous books include *Foreign Plaintiffs in Products Liability Actions, Frivolous Lawsuits and Frivolous Defenses, Federal Statutes on Environmental Protection, The Right of Privacy in the Computer Age*, and *Professional Sports and Antitrust*, all published by Quorum Books.